VOL

MACRO-ECONOMIC POLICY
IN AUSTRALIA

MACRO-ECONOMIC POLICY
IN AUSTRALIA

SECOND EDITION

J. O. N. Perkins

Professor of Economics
University of Melbourne

MELBOURNE UNIVERSITY PRESS
1975

First published 1971
Second Edition 1975

Printed in Australia by
Alexander Bros Pty Ltd, Mentone, Victoria 3194, for
Melbourne University Press, Carlton, Victoria 3053
USA and Canada: ISBS Inc., Portland, Oregon 97208
Great Britain, Europe, the Middle East, Africa and the Caribbean:
International Book Distributors Ltd (Prentice-Hall International),
66 Wood Lane End, Hemel Hempstead,
Hertfordshire HP2 4RG, England

National Library of Australia
Cataloguing in Publication data

Perkins, James Oliver Newton
  Macro-economic policy in Australia/[by] J. O. N.
  Perkins.–2nd ed.—Carlton, Vic.: Melbourne Univer-
  sity Press, 1975.
  Includes bibliographical references.
  ISBN 0 522 84089 2
  1. Monetary policy–Australia–History.
  2. Fiscal policy–Australia–History.
  I. Title.
  339.50994.

Contents

Preface to First Edition

This survey of the principal macro-economic problems and policies of the Australian economy in recent years analyses the experience and the main lessons of the 1960s and, in much less detail, those of the 1950s. It includes most of the material on the period 1960–66 from an earlier study *Anti-cyclical Policy in Australia, 1960–1966*.

The author is indebted to many colleagues who have at one time or another read and provided comments on various parts of the preliminary drafts. These include Professor K. A. Blakey, Dr E. A. Boehm, Professor R. F. Henderson, Mr R. S. Jones, Mr D. M. Mahoney, Mr J. E. Sullivan and Professor W. Prest. Responsibility for remaining deficiencies is of course my own.

Miss D. Bremanis and Miss E. B. Williamson gave valuable assistance with the collation of relevant statistical material from the data bank of the Institute of Applied Economic and Social Research, University of Melbourne.

The secretarial staff of the University of Melbourne Department of Economics, especially Mrs J. Vike and Miss M. Jacobsen, managed the typing with admirable efficiency.

October 1970   J.O.N.P.

Preface to the Second Edition

This edition extends the material in the first edition to cover the experience of the period between 1970 and 1974. It has benefited considerably from the comments of a number of academics and Reserve Bank economists. A special word of thanks is due to Mr R. H. Wallace of the Flinders University of South Australia for his many very helpful suggestions, and to Dr N. R. Norman of the University of Melbourne. None of these is of course responsible for remaining deficiencies.

Dr Norman has given valuable assistance by preparing the tables and graphs.

March 1975   J.O.N.P.

*To the policy-makers—who
must be sick of armchair critics.*

Introduction

This survey discusses Australia's experience in the field of macro-economic policies, principally during the years 1960–74. That is to say, it is concerned with those policy decisions that relate to the maintenance of full employment without undue inflation (the policy objective known as 'internal balance') and an adequately strong balance of payments ('external balance').

The area of policy under discussion might perhaps be more accurately described as that of short-run macro-economic policy, for the discussion will not be concerned with such matters as immigration policy or other measures that relate primarily to the long-run economic potential of the economy.

The term 'anti-cyclical' or 'counter-cyclical' might perhaps have been employed (as in an earlier study by the present writer) to delimit the area of policy under discussion. But the use of such a term might be taken to imply that the nature of the problems being encountered is necessarily of a regularly cyclical nature, and that the mere elimination of cyclical fluctuations should be the aim; whereas in fact the appropriate aim is the achievement of a steady rate of economic growth *at a high level of economic activity.* The broader term 'macro-economic' policy has therefore been preferred, even though the term 'macro-economic' is not yet common currency in everyday speech. But it has become very widely used in discussions of economic issues in recent years, and there is no exact equivalent for it in more general use. It refers simply to those aspects of economic policy that are concerned with aggregates—the overall level of demand and of the balance of payments (for 'macro' means 'large'), as distinct from the smaller-scale ('micro') aspects of the economy, such as the activities of particular firms or industries.

These overall, aggregative aspects of policy may thus be usefully distinguished from those concerned with the allocation of resources or the distribution of income. It is true that the distribution of income and the allocation of resources will be affected by the particular combination of macro-economic measures chosen, and that such effects (where they can be foreseen) will normally be taken into account in deciding what combination of measures to adopt; it is, however, both more convenient, and more usual, to consider the impact of macro-economic policy measures on the overall objectives of internal and external balance separately from these other aspects of policy, and this will be the approach adopted in this survey.

One of the principal weapons of policy available to the government for achieving internal and external balance is budgetary policy. This relates to the level of government expenditure and of transfer payments such as pensions, together with tax receipts. The other main measures are those of monetary policy: these include not only the monetary effects of the budget itself, but also official operations in the market for government securities, and interest-rate policy generally, together with the various weapons that influence bank lending and the activities of other financial institutions.[1] But in addition the rate of exchange (the price at which Australian dollars can be converted into other currencies) affects both internal and external balance, as does also the general level of tariffs and any controls over imports (such as existed during the period up to 1960) and over other external payments.

There is little discussion in this study of prices and incomes policies, for these have played only a minor (or even a negligible) role in Australia, at least until recently. The aim of such policies is to try to keep the rise in money incomes per head as close as possible to the growth in real output per head: for otherwise inflation may be intolerably rapid, even if demand (in money terms) does not rise faster than the capacity of the economy at full employment. Or, alternatively, if such a condition of rising prices occurs, governments may feel obliged—whether for domestic or external reasons—to tolerate a lower level of activity and economic growth (and higher level of unemployment) than would otherwise be thought tolerable, in the hope of thus checking the inflation. The solution of the complex and crucial questions of incomes policy is thus probably vital to a successful solution of the problems of internal and external balance. But some would argue that if excess demand ('overall employment') is avoided, problems of cost inflation will not be serious: and whether or not this is so, it remains true that the problems of internal and external balance require the pursuit of appropriate budgetary and monetary policies,

[1] The present study assumes that the reader will have a basic understanding of the way monetary policy operates in Australia, and of the various factors that influence bank lending and the money supply, and of how these influence activity in the capital market and the level of demand. These are analysed in J. O. N. Perkins and J. E. Sullivan, *Banks and the Capital Market* (Melbourne, 1972).

even assuming that an appropriate incomes policy can be achieved.[2] Obviously, decisions of Arbitration Commissions and everything else that influences incomes and prices also affect the balance of payments and the extent of unemployment or overfull employment. At the same time, measures of budgetary and monetary policy affect the general level of prices as well as the level of demand relative to capacity. But governments can probably do little to influence the course of wages and prices in the short run, except through the influence of their monetary and budgetary policies on the general level of demand. In Australia the evidence on behalf of the government at hearings of the Arbitration Commission is the most practicable form of direct governmental influence on wage-rates and incomes per head in general, and its potential importance should not be ignored. It should also be remembered that government policy for the control of monopolies and restrictive practices, and in tariffs and subsidies, also affects the general level of prices.

The main reason for studying Australia's past experience in the field of macro-economic policy is for the light it may shed on the sort of problems that are likely to be faced in future, and on appropriate ways of dealing with them. In particular, the experience of the fairly recent past is generally likely to be the most relevant, because the setting in which policy will have to operate in future is likely to resemble fairly closely that of the past decade or so, whereas it may well be very different from that prevailing twenty years earlier. For example,

[2] Some aspects of these problems are discussed in J. E. Isaac, *Wages and Productivity* (Melbourne, 1967); chapter 7 of *Report of the Committee of Economic Enquiry* (the 'Vernon' Report) (Canberra, 1965); chapter 39 of P. A. Samuelson, K. Hancock and R. H. Wallace, *Economics* (Australian ed., Sydney, 1970); and chapter 9 of E. A. Boehm, *Twentieth Century Economic Development in Australia* (Melbourne, 1971).

the very rapid growth and the increasing complexity of the institutions of the Australian capital market during the 1960s radically changed the setting for monetary policy compared with that of the 1950s. Another important change was that the major additional policy weapon of import controls which was available during the 1950s was not in fact used in the 1960s, and it is reasonable to assume that it will probably not be available in future: this consideration therefore also makes the experience of the 1950s to that extent less relevant to the future than is that of the period since 1960.

For such reasons as these, the discussion of this book is centred mainly on the 1960s and 1970–4, with an eye to assessing their likely relevance for future policy decisions. Nevertheless, it seems worth while first to review, in a much more summary way, some of the principal features of the experience of the 1950s. For the success of macro-economic measures during the greater part of the 1960s probably owed a good deal to lessons learned during the 1950s; whilst some of the principal policy instruments used in the 1960s were evolved in the earlier period.

The use of budgetary policy to influence the level of effective demand was gradually accepted and established during the 1950s, even though the timing of budgetary measures at some critical junctures left a good deal to be desired. In particular, the very high level of effective demand in 1950/1—which resulted largely from the enormous rise in export receipts during the Korean War—was not offset by appropriate anti-inflationary budgetary measures until late in 1951, when the boom was virtually over. Moreover, the very sharp rise in the supplies of imports that occurred in 1951/2 was tending to reduce the demand for domestic output in that period, so that the tax increases of the 1951 budget were so timed that their main effect was to intensify the subsequent recession.

In the same way, during the next period of excess demand, which was centred on 1955, adequate steps to restrain demand were not taken until early in 1956, when the boom was again past its peak; and on this occasion also these measures therefore tended to intensify the subsequent lapse from full employment.

In much the same way, anti-inflationary monetary measures were not applied soon enough or on a sufficient scale in 1950 and 1955 to prevent the occurrence of excess demand. Bond prices were supported by the central bank in these periods and, partly as a result of these official bond purchases, the money supply was allowed to rise unduly sharply and interest rates were not raised soon enough to prevent excess demand from occurring. When at last those interest rates under official control were permitted to rise, and when (at about the same time) bank lending was successfully restrained, the downward impact of these monetary measures upon demand came rather too late and so contributed to keeping demand below full employment in 1952/3 and 1957/8. But in considering the use made of monetary policy one must bear in mind the difficulties that the central bank had in forging reliable weapons of control over the rate of bank lending (the main form of monetary policy employed in that period); for a firm convention that the banks would keep the minimum ratio of their 'L.G.S.' assets to deposits at a stated figure (originally 14 per cent, and later raised to 16 per cent and then 18 per cent) came to be accepted by the banks only in the late 1950s—well after the two periods of boom during that decade.

When budgetary and monetary measures were employed during the 1950s to restrain domestic demand, the intention was both to eliminate excess demand and to improve the balance of payments (by curtailing imports through the restraint on domestic expenditure). For in 1951/2 and 1955/6 the balance of payments deficits were such that urgent measures were needed to effect such an improvement. But from 1952 onwards the weapon of general import controls also was used to keep imports at a level that could be financed from the prevailing level of exports and capital inflow; these controls were therefore tightened during the periods of maximum strain on the country's international reserves (in 1952, when they were imposed, and then 1955), and they were relaxed in the intervening periods. The policy-makers thus tried to vary the combinations of monetary and budgetary measures on the one hand and import controls on the other in such a way as to achieve as close an approach as possible to internal and external balance, even though the flexibility and timing of their policy variations were often open to criticism.

The predominant background to macro-economic policy during most of the 1950s was anxiety about the balance of payments: the absence of this besetting worry during most of the 1960s therefore constituted a basic difference between the general macro-economic problems facing the policy-makers during each of these two periods. But the fluctuations in the level of domestic activity over the two decades followed a remarkably similar pattern, the peak levels of activity being in 1950, 1955, 1960, 1964/5 and 1969/70; so that these peaks more or less coincided with the years at the beginning and in the middle of the decades; and between each of the peaks there were periods in which the economy was operating, to varying degrees, at less than full employment. But, with the important exception of the recession of 1961–2, the fluctuations in the level of unemployment, and the actual level of unemployment, were during the 1960s generally less than they had been in earlier years.

During the 1960s, Australia faced in turn each of the possible combinations of problems of internal and external balance; inflation and balance of payments deficit in 1960; recession and balance of payments deficit in 1961; less than full employment with a balance of payments surplus in 1962–3 and 1966; and balance of payments surplus with full (or with a tendency to over-full) employment in 1964–5 and 1969–70.[3]

A study of this period may thus be taken as an illustrated guide to general discussion of these issues; and the lessons of each of the phases of this period should shed some light on any future set of problems in these fields of overall economic policy. Of course, every period has special aspects peculiar to itself; but the general framework in which the problems and policies of internal and external balance can be discussed may be adapted to any situation that arises. At the same time, an examination of actual cases may often be more helpful, particularly to the general reader or average informed voter, than a consideration of the various possible combinations of problems and policies in the abstract.

During the years 1970–4 much more serious macro-

[3] The term 'balance of payments surplus' may be used to mean merely an addition to the country's reserves; but from the point of view of policy its most useful meaning is 'a stronger balance of payments than the country would wish to continue indefinitely'. The former of these two meanings certainly applied to the periods 1962–3, 1963–4 and 1969–70. Whether the policy sense of the term was also applicable is a matter of opinion. But at the very least one may suppose that wide agreement could be reached that the immediate balance of payments outlook in 1962–4 and in 1969–70 was certainly not uncomfortably weak.

economic problems arose than had typified the 1950s and 1960s, in the sense that the early 1970s were marked by a much higher rate of inflation than at any time since the Korean War in 1950/1, and 1974 saw a combination of these much higher rates of inflation with a higher level of unemployment than at any time since the 1930s. This new combination of high unemployment and high inflation was virtually world-wide and certainly not peculiar to Australia. So far, neither policy in any of the major countries nor the available economic literature has proved apt for handling these new and very serious problems.

It continues to be important to remember and apply the lessons of the 1950s and 1960s, which have considerable relevance for the basic macro-economic problems of maintaining an adequate but not excessive level of demand, and a satisfactory state of the balance of payments. But the equally crucial aim must now be to achieve these aims with a minimum rate of inflation, at any given level of activity. If the basic aims are to be achieved without an intolerable rate of inflation, then the focus of attention of policy-makers and commentators (and the electorate generally) must equally be focused on the precise combination of measures (the 'policy mix') with which the aims of internal and external balance are achieved; for some alternatives will clearly be more likely than others to raise the rate of inflation at any given level of activity. In particular, as we shall see, this means readiness to accept nominal interest rates that would in the past have been considered high, readiness to reduce tax rates, reluctance to devalue, willingness to reduce tariffs wherever possible, and a slower rate of expansion of government spending than one would otherwise have preferred.

In short, the main thesis of this book is that we must

not forget the lessons of the 1950s and the 1960s about maintaining internal and external balance. But we must now add to them the new lessons based on the years 1970–4, especially those that relate to choosing the most appropriate 'policy mix' for restraining inflation at any given level of activity.

The following are the principal questions to be considered in the analysis of each of the various phases into which the period can be divided:

(i) What were the main problems of internal and external balance facing the policy-makers?

(ii) What were the principal measures taken to deal with them (and the principal omissions)?

(iii) How successful were the measures taken?

(iv) What lessons can be drawn from this experience?

1960: Boom and External Deficit

The year 1960 was characterized by a rising level of total demand relative to capacity, though excess demand was heavily concentrated upon a few areas—principally motor vehicles and building (mainly dwellings)—and it is thus a matter of opinion and definition whether it is strictly exact to describe the general state of the economy as being one of 'overfull employment'. However, the tendency for prices to rise and for 'inflationary psychology'—the expectation of further price rises—to take hold, showing itself in the unhealthy boom in real estate and share prices, gave cause for concern. In other words, even if the authorities did not accept the view that the labour market was becoming so tight as to necessitate measures to remove excess demand, there can be little doubt that the need to check inflationary expectations would have tipped the balance eventually in the direction of taking measures to check the rise in total demand relative to capacity.

In any event, the decisive consideration was probably that of external balance, for by November the reserves were falling to a level and at a rate that the government could not have permitted to continue—if only because a point could otherwise have been reached at which serious speculation on the possibility of a devaluation of the Australian pound might have occurred, and the consequent capital outflow would then have rendered the position intolerable. It is true that part of the rise in imports could be interpreted as a once-for-all effect of the removal of the import controls, as new sources of supply were tapped and as new products were bought for the first time. Moreover, the state of the reserves inevitably prompted fears of the restoration of the import controls, and this may have caused a once-for-all rise in imports on this account also. It seems that the fairly tight credit situation in Australia did not have much effect in restricting imports. This was in part associated with the big rise in short-term capital inflow over the period; apparently importers raised more of the finance for the imports from overseas, and on longer terms, than usual. Although it is true that this cushioned the impact upon the reserves of the rise in imports, it also meant that the monetary measures taken were less effective in checking imports (and perhaps also in checking domestic demand—in so far as the availability of credit from overseas directly or indirectly replaced credit that would otherwise have been sought within the country).

Measures prior to November 1960

The measures taken during the course of the first half of 1960 to check inflation were: first, the removal of import controls; second, central bank efforts to bring about a progressive tightening of bank credit, by calls to Statutory Reserve Deposits and instructions to banks to curtail their new lending; third, the 'intervention' by the government in the basic wage case of that year, in the unprecedented form of a clear statement of the government's view that a further rise in wage levels was undesirable in the present state of the economy.

The virtually complete removal of import controls

brought to an end a process of relaxation that had been going on for some time. The government's view—perfectly logical in itself—was that the freer availability of imports would absorb some of the inflationary forces at work in the economy. It may also have seemed that if the controls were ever to be removed this was the time to do it. It may be remembered that when imposed eight years before they had been considered as 'temporary'; it would obviously become increasingly difficult in future to present them as such. In view of the criticisms that were later levelled at the decision to remove the controls, it seems necessary to emphasize that in itself the decision was justified. What was open to criticism was the failure to keep the rise in domestic demand down to a level that the country's internal and external resources would warrant.

The progressive tightening of bank credit was a necessary part of the anti-inflationary measures, but—almost incredibly—for the third boom in succession efforts to curb bank lending were offset by a bond support policy that committed the central bank to intervening in the bond market to prevent interest rates rising (that is, bond prices from falling) as much as would otherwise have occurred.[1] This official support for the bond market was removed only in November, when the damage had been done and the boom was almost over: the peak in the economy had already passed. The failure to permit a rise in bond rates or in bank fixed-interest-bearing deposit rates (beyond a small increase early in 1960) meant that lending to non-bank financial intermediaries

[1] The small and gradual rises in rates permitted at the short end of the market (referred to in H. W. Arndt and C. P. Harris, *The Australian Trading Banks* (Melbourne, 1964), p. 206) may have made matters worse, in that they probably strengthened expectations that yields would eventually rise to a higher level, so reducing the incentive to hold bonds.

and directly to trading companies continued to be relatively attractive to the public. The consequent 'activation of idle deposits' brought a higher level of private spending than could have been supported by a given money supply if the banks had been permitted to offer higher rates on interest-bearing deposits (and so become more competitive borrowers of idle funds). Moreover, any rise in overdraft rates would have had some effect in curbing the demand for overdrafts and the willingness of bank customers to use their overdraft limits more fully. The argument that a small rise would do little good in this direction may be true, but it is in a sense irrelevant; for any rise would have helped. It is true of course that with an expectation of a general rise in prices of the order of 3 to 4 per cent per annum, a substantial rise in overdraft rates would have been necessary to raise to a deterrent level the cost of what was—in real terms—almost interest-free bank credit. For interest rates remained very low, if calculated in terms of the expected real value of the money in which the loans and interest would have to be repaid in future. It is not suggested that borrowers actually consider the facts in exactly this way: it is merely that in periods of inflationary expectations the prospects for a high money rate of profits appear exceedingly strong; and money that can be borrowed at a nominal rate of, say, 5 per cent appears therefore to be very attractive in such periods. The conclusion must be that a small but significant rise in those interest rates under official control should usually be permitted before inflationary expectations get a grip; certainly the efficacy of monetary policy must be impaired if increases in official and bank interest rates are permitted to lag behind those being paid in the capital market generally.

The government intervention in the basic wage case

presumably had some influence on the Arbitration Commission's decision to refrain from granting further wage increases in 1960. But after the extraordinary rise in money incomes following the basic wage and margins decisions of 1959, it would presumably have been clear to the commission, even without such a forthright government statement, that further general and widespread increases would have increased the risk of serious inflation—and so the risk of the government having to take drastic action to check demand.

As to budgetary measures, the 1960/1 budget announced in August took some anti-inflationary action by way of higher taxes on personal incomes and companies. What was needed most, however, was a psychological blow to dampen excess business optimism. A forthright statement of the government's determination to do whatever was necessary to check the boom (preferably reinforced by an appropriate interest-rate policy) was needed; but it was conspicuously lacking in the Treasurer's budget statement. Had it formed the key part of such a statement the measures actually brought down might conceivably have sufficed; though preferably some such measures should have been adopted earlier. The passing of the peak of the share boom shortly afterwards (in September) suggests that such a statement might have struck at the psychological moment. Certainly, such an approach coupled with an appropriate interest-rate policy might well have obviated the need for the measures of November 1960, and thus have reduced the extent of the loss of potential output during the subsequent recession.

By mid-November it seemed to the government that the measures taken earlier in the year had not been adequate to check either the balance of payments deficit or the forces of domestic inflation; or, at any rate, it was felt that the evidence was not sufficient for it to be reasonably sure that the peak demand and peak imports had passed, though some observers felt at the time that in fact forces were already at work to check the rise in imports and the rise in total demand, and some fall in imports was expected, in any event, once the peak of re-stocking was passed.

It is not possible to assess the relative importance of domestic and external considerations in influencing the government's decision to introduce a new package deal of anti-inflationary measures. In any case, the two groups of considerations were in some measure intertwined. The drawing and stand-by loan from the International Monetary Fund (I.M.F.) were negotiated on the understanding that appropriate measures would be taken to curb inflation, though the government affirmed (and there is no reason to disbelieve the statement) that the policy measures it adopted were those it would have chosen in any event, quite apart from the negotiations with the I.M.F.

The measures of November 1960

In appraising the November 1960 measures in retrospect we must bear in mind the circumstances in which they were taken. To repeat, the situation was such that there could be no reasonable confidence that the measures already taken would suffice to arrest the fall in the reserves and to remove the danger of overfull employment and an undesirable degree of inflation. Further delay in checking the boom was thought likely to intensify the reaction when it did eventually occur. One may of course argue that this situation should not have been allowed to arise; that more appropriate policy decisions should have been taken earlier in the year—though the swift change from inadequate to excess demand between 1959 and 1960 afforded some defence for the policy-makers. But something further probably had to be done in the light of knowledge available in November 1960, even if in retrospect the policy may appear to have been misguided. Moreover, nearly all the measures announced at that time (several of which were never enforced, or only in a modified form) were in fact of a sort well calculated to have a sharp psychological effect and, with one important exception, to be quickly reversible if need be.

There was first a drastic reinforcement of the credit squeeze, in the shape of a sharply-worded injunction to the banks to reduce the level of their advances. This seems to have resulted in an actual calling in of credit—probably at about the time when the progressive tightening of new lending earlier in the year was beginning to have its main effect. Coupled with this was a very belated raising of those interest rates under official control—bond rates (the short rate rising above the long for most of the first half of 1961) and bank interest rates—which reinforced the credit squeeze by making bank borrowing more expensive and also by making it relatively more attractive than it had been to hold fixed-interest-bearing deposits with banks, rather than to lend to non-bank financial intermediaries.[2]

After November, the fall in bond prices, coupled with and intensifying the break in the share and real estate markets that had already occurred, had an adverse effect on confidence generally. People were no longer ready, and even anxious, to lend (which they had been during

[2] The long-term bond rate went up from 5 per cent to just over 5¼ per cent. The maximum overdraft rate was raised from 6 per cent to 7 per cent, but the average rate charged was to rise only from 5½ per cent to 6 per cent. The maximum fixed-interest deposit rate (now to be on deposits for twelve instead of twenty-four months) was raised to 4½ per cent.

most of 1960), for the credit-worthiness of borrowers was no longer accepted so readily; whilst the difficulty now expected, and experienced, in obtaining bank and non-bank credit led to a general movement to conserve and obtain liquidity.

The government could not have known how great a blow to confidence it was precipitating, and would presumably have preferred (in the light of hindsight) to have done something less drastic; for the oficial measures came at a time when the natural course of events was probably also working in the same direction, as could be seen subsequently. The real criticism of the monetary measures is that they did not come sooner, or at least that interest rates were not raised sooner, for it is true that the efforts to curb bank lending had been in progress for several months.

There is a danger that the natural public reaction to the November 1960 measures may at some future time of strain on the economy make it politically difficult to impose tight monetary measures when they are need—for fear of the now odious term 'credit squeeze' being applied to the measures. (There were signs that this situation might arise in 1963–4 as a result of the 1963 and 1964 election campaigns, and even some suggestions of such an attitude during the period of tight money in 1970.) If a government were ever hampered by such a widespread misinterpretation of the events of 1960, this would of course increase the risk of the same course of events being repeated; for failure to apply the measures of tighter credit early in a boom might again make it necessary to have recourse to really drastic measures too late to do anything but intensify the down-swing.

The fiscal measures introduced in November 1960 were either never in fact applied or else quickly reversed

—with the important exception of that relating to insurance companies and pension funds. The intention was announced of making interest paid on fixed-interest borrowing by companies (above its level in some base period) no longer tax deductible. Though this was never applied, the expectation that it would be introduced was one factor leading many finance companies to reduce the scale of their business (especially by withdrawing from the field of real estate into which they had expanded during 1960 and earlier), as it would have greatly increased the cost of their borrowing and so reduced the scope for them to earn profits. In any case, the supply of funds to finance companies dropped sharply as firms and individuals sought greater liquidity; and the demand for hire-purchase facilities fell away sharply at the same time, partly because of the rise in sales-tax on cars (from 30 per cent to 40 per cent). Interest paid on new issues of convertible notes (fixed-interest obligations that could later be converted into shares) was in fact made no longer tax deductible; but this was a minor measure, though it appreciably reduced the scope for small firms to secure development finance, and was thus of questionable value from a long-term viewpoint.

The rise in the sales-tax on cars was important and effective, as it concentrated the anti-inflationary effect on the demand for the products of an industry that was unquestionably overstrained, and which was also one important cause of the very sharp rise in imports during the year. If powers to control hire-purchase lending had been available, there can be little doubt that they would have been applied—perhaps even instead of a rise in the sales-tax. Whatever the advantages and disadvantages or difficulties of direct controls over hire-purchase in general, there can be no doubt that increases in taxes on those consumer durables in excess demand are more likely to be effective, as they reduce cash sales as well as those on terms. It may be added that so far as the demand for the products of other consumer-durables industries may not be excessive at the time, the more discriminatory sales-tax weapon may be preferable, since any enforced tightening of hire-purchase terms in general would be likely to reduce demand for all consumer durables financed by hire-purchase.

It is true that the concentration of hire-purchase controls upon reducing demand for the products of 'growth' industries—which are usually the ones that expand most in times of high activity—has been criticized (in countries applying such controls) as tending to prevent the consumer from exercising his preference for raising his consumption of durable goods especially sharply when he finds his income rising; and also as tending to reduce the incentive for industry to expand capacity in those industries whose products are in strongest demand as living standards rise.

However, so far as the demand for the products in question is clearly in excess of the capacity of the durables industries, and also in excess of the long-term trend level, measures to lop off the top of the boom in demand for these products should help to stabilize demand for the products over the good and bad years together. Swift reductions of taxes imposed in the boom should contribute to the achievement of this and ensure that adequate incentive remains to expand the capacity of these industries in line with the long-run trend in demand for these products.

The speed with which the government reduced the sales-tax on cars—in early 1961—was therefore commendable. But in this case the general reduction in business confidence and the down-swing in employment and incomes caused the demand for cars to remain slack for nearly another year.

One other measure proposed in November 1960—to compel insurance companies and pension funds to hold a certain proportion of their assets in the form of government and semi-government bonds—was never imposed in that form, but instead there was later introduced the so-called '30/20' provision which gave a strong tax incentive to these institutions to build up their holdings of government bonds to the point where their total holdings of government and semi-government bonds was equal to 30 per cent of their assets, and within this total to hold an amount equal to 20 per cent of their total assets in Commonwealth bonds.

Whatever may be said for and against such measures on general long-term grounds, in the present context of anti-cyclical policy the measures were open to strong criticism in their timing. It was not merely that like the other November 1960 measures they applied an anti-inflationary (and indeed deflationary) influence at a time when the boom was passing, but that in this case their main impact was actually delayed until about the worst part of the recession. For the consequent adjustment over that period of the portfolios of the companies and funds that were affected meant that they bought more government bonds (presumably, mainly by subscribing more than they otherwise would have done, and so increasing the total of bond sales by the government) in a period when this was the opposite of the appropriate policy. For it tended to reduce bank liquidity and that of the public generally, so that bank as well as certain non-bank lenders had less available to lend to the private sector, especially for housing. Even if one accepts that such a tax-incentive is a defensible way of encouraging bond subscriptions as an anti-inflationary measure in times of boom such as 1960, the imposition of such a lasting (instead of an anti-cyclical) inducement to effect such a transfer of funds to the government, at a time when its effects would obviously be felt after the boom had passed, was—from the point of view of macro-economic policy—a cardinal error. One might argue perhaps that its introduction could pave the way for cyclically variable measures of a similar sort in future; but apart from the problems of portfolio adjustment that this would imply for the institutions concerned, this would be a cumbersome and less effective way of achieving the aim in view than an appropriately flexible policy of interest rates and debt management. The only point one can make in favour of this measure introduced in November 1960 is that it was somewhat less objectionable—though not much different in its effects—than compelling the institutions to hold a stated proportion of their assets in the form of bonds, as had originally been proposed. (Unfortunately, the tax incentive it gives for the institutions in question to hold bonds firmly may make them favour its continuance; obviously, a more flexible debt policy on the part of the government would face the institutions concerned with greater problems of portfolio management—and the Treasury with more complex problems of debt policy—than does the permanent application of the '30/20' ratio.)

Lessons of the 1960 'credit squeeze'

The difficulties of securing an appropriate reduction in bank lending during 1960 suggest some lessons for the future.[3] Apart from the failure (until November) to raise

[3] These have been admirably analysed by R. W. Davis and R. H. Wallace in 'Lessons of the 1960 "Credit Squeeze" ', *Australian Economic Papers*, June 1963.

permitted overdraft rates to more appropriate levels, there was the problem arising from the fact that, as the actual L.G.S. (liquid assets plus government securities to deposits) ratios of different banks varied considerably one from another, a sufficiently severe policy of calls to S.R.D.s (Statutory Reserve Deposits) to reduce the most liquid bank's L.G.S. ratio to near the agreed minimum was likely to have too severe an effect upon those banks with lower initial L.G.S. ratios; whereas discrimination as between banks in respect of the amounts (expressed as a percentage of their deposit liabilities) called to S.R.D.s was not possible.[4] An alternative has been suggested of making calls to S.R.D.s on such a scale as to compel even the most liquid bank to reduce its lending, coupled with loans from the central bank on easy terms to those banks with lower initial liquidity (so that they would not have to bear more than their proportionate share of the curtailment of lending).[5] This might be worth considering for the future. But in any case the L.G.S. minimum was not statutory and might have been ignored by the banks in the event of very harsh calls to S.R.D.s. Powers to make it statutorily enforceable, if this should prove necessary, might reasonably be taken for the future. There was also the problem that the agreement about the L.G.S. ratio related to the seasonal minimum; at other periods of the year a figure well below the level consistent with a seasonal minimum at the agreed figure might be reached without the bank needing to reduce its lending or to borrow from the central bank. The suggestion that the banks should declare seasonal adjustment factors for their L.G.S. ratios (and

[4] It was ruled out by law under the legislation that came into force in early 1960; but in any case it had not been practised for many years before that and would have been politically difficult even if considered workable and desirable in itself.

[5] See Davis and Wallace, op. cit.

borrow where necessary to maintain these at all times) might be worth considering.[6] But, in fact, the control by way of the agreed minimum L.G.S. ratio seems to have worked well during the 1960s, even though at any given time there have usually been some banks with an L.G.S. ratio appreciably above the agreed minimum.

Certain banks appear to have had to borrow from the Reserve Bank during 1960 (and into 1961) to maintain the agreed minimum L.G.S. ratios. As in the previous boom, the growth of non-bank credit both made it more necessary for the Reserve Bank to try to obtain a curtailment of lending by banks and also, naturally, made the banks far from eager to conform with such requests in view of the profits they saw being earned by the unrestricted 'second banking system' or 'fringe banking institutions'—as they were described. A more enlightened interest-rate policy would have reduced the extent of this growth of non-bank credit. Whether or not it would also have been desirable and expedient to take powers of direct control over the non-bank intermediaries is a complex matter.[7] It is certainly not an issue that can be decided—as some writers seem almost to suggest at times—by mere reference to the fact that they were 'uncontrolled'. At the same time, if appropriately used (and if it were found or made constitutionally possible), some form of control over the liquidity of finance companies or any companies borrowing for short periods at fixed interest, or over the terms of consumer credit, might prove useful in helping to maintain economic stability at some future time. However, if an unforeseen expansion of non-bank credit does occur in another boom it is quite likely that it will take some totally different form, and the greater the

[6] Ibid.
[7] It is discussed below (pp. 111–14).

powers available to control particular forms of non-bank credit expansion, the more likely is it that other, uncontrolled forms will be devised which would not be subject to such limitations.

The 1961 Recession and External Deficit

During the course of 1961 the economy passed into a mild but definite recession, the trough of which was reached in the September quarter (on the evidence of most indicators). From an internal point of view there was clearly scope—and need—for the expansion of demand. Externally there was still some cause for anxiety, for by the middle of 1961 reserves remained low, although they were beginning to recover and imports had fallen to much more tolerable levels. In addition, exports showed some appreciable increases and private capital inflow was at a remarkably high level. It thus proved possible for the drawing that was made on the International Monetary Fund in April 1961 to be repaid in early 1962, but the need to build up the reserves to a healthier level meant that the external picture was still one of 'deficit' in the policy sense (of a weaker balance of payments than the country needed to achieve).

Such monetary measures to stimulate domestic demand as were taken during 1961 consisted mainly of a gradual relaxation, from about mid-1961, of the pressure on banks to keep down their lending, and a reduction in their S.R.D.s; but in the situation of low business confidence it was not surprising that this apparently had little effect. Measures were also taken to cushion the fall

in the supply of finance for housing, especially that from
finance companies, by providing extra funds to the states
from the Commonwealth and also through the banking
system. But monetary policy during this period did not
include any general reduction in bank and official interest rates. Moreover, it must be borne in mind that the
inflationary expectations of 1960 had by now given way
to the expectation of something like price stability. In
real terms, therefore, bond rates and bank interest rates
were actually well above those prevailing even after the
increases in November 1960.[1]

It might of course reasonably be argued that reductions in interest rates would have had little effect in
stimulating demand in a period of widespread excess
capacity. But the expectation that the next movement in
interest rates would probably be downwards must have
represented some inducement to businesses to postpone
expenditure until borrowing terms became more attractive. In actual fact, there was a minor reduction in
the long-term bond rate in the last quarter of
1961—from the peak of over 5¼ per cent to which it
was raised in November 1960 to just below 5 per cent,
the level at which it had stood throughout the boom up
to November 1960. But such a gradual and hesitant
reduction was in marked contrast to what was
required; for the expectation of further reductions gave a
strong inducement to banks, to other financial institutions, and indeed to individuals, to build up their

---

[1] The reduction of ¼ per cent in the banks' maximum fixed-
interest-bearing deposit rate in June 1961 was accompanied by a rise
of ¼ per cent in the savings banks' deposit rates. It must thus be
regarded as an adjustment of relative rates offered by different parts
of the banking system—presumably in part to facilitate extra lending
for housing by the savings banks by attracting deposits to them—
rather than as a measure of general monetary policy.

holdings of government bonds, rather than their lending to the private sector (for example, for housing).

The growing liquidity of the economy during 1961–2 seems to have been one reason for the hesitation of the authorities in taking more expansionary action. They seem to have feared a return to something nearer to the 1960 readiness of business to increase its indebtedness, and of lenders to forgo liquidity; and that the high level of liquidity might become the basis of a dangerously sharp rise in spending. But the blow to business confidence of the November 1960 measures was not so soon rectified. Business was not anxious to undertake new investment programmes now that there was so much spare capacity in existence; and, even if it had wished to expand capacity further, the shocks of the past year or so were such that firms and individuals were not likely to be able or willing to incur debt or to lend on the scale and terms that had proved feasible in 1960.

But the authorities' actions to stimulate demand remained cautious. The 1961 budget contained minor concessions in sales-tax, and some social services benefits were also increased. It is true, however, that public works expenditure was increased—mainly through extra grants to the states—on a scale that clearly had in mind the need for reflationary measures. But these had their main effect only in 1962 and non-official observers at the time felt the measures inadequate; and so it proved.

In February 1962, therefore, the Treasurer restored the 5 per cent rebate on income tax for 1962–3, to be effective entirely in the remaining four months of the financial year—in effect a reduction of 15 per cent in income tax liabilities for these four months, which was intended to give an immediate sharp stimulus to spending. There were also more increases in public expenditure and further sales-tax reductions. In addition, there were concessions to industry by way of investment allowances, which were, apparently, expected to stimulate private investment.

The improvement in the economy left activity well short of full employment. Private investment revived only gradually, though expenditure on motor vehicles played a principal role in leading the recovery, partly under the stimulus of the sales-tax reduction of February 1961.

Rising exports helped to provide some stimulus to demand and brought a further improvement in the balance of payments, especially as imports did not in this period recover in step with the recovery of the economy. With the drawing from the I.M.F. now repaid, and with reserves now back at about the level at which it had been thought safe to remove import controls in 1960, one may regard the period of external deficit (in the policy sense) as having passed. From about mid-1962, therefore, the external situation may be thought of as one of approximate balance—not unduly strong and not unduly weak.

Lessons of the recession

The principal conclusion about policy in 1961 must be that action to stimulate demand was reluctant, belated and inadequate in circumstances where the prevalence of excess capacity made it both desirable and feasible to take bold and timely action to revive demand. The further an economy is from full employment the safer and more necessary is it to risk erring, if at all, on the side of giving too great a boost to spending. In retrospect, it seems extraordinary that an official fear of precipitating (in totally different circumstances) a revival of the inflationary attitudes of 1960 should have apparently inhibited the government from implementing adequate expansionary action. Moreover, such monetary action as it did take in 1961 was almost solely through bank credit (almost useless as a stimulus in a recession if unsupported by adequate other measures) and with virtually no reduction in interest rates (which might at least have given some stimulus to the depressed housebuilding sector). Moreover, budgetary measures also turned out to be inadequate.

Colour is lent to this criticism by the commendable flexibility of budgetary policy in 1962 (even though this, too, turned out to be insufficiently expansionary), since this showed what would presumably have been feasible earlier in the recession. The alteration of effective income tax rates twice—so that in effect three different scales were applicable within a period of five months—indicates that this weapon had been found to have a degree of flexibility not hitherto thought to be administratively feasible (either in Australia or, so far as the present writer is aware, in any other country). The provision of additional grants to the states, including some to stimulate housing and some directed towards alleviating unemployment where it was worst, also indicates lines on which action might usefully be applied in a more timely and discriminating manner in any similar circumstances in future. One may hope that advance plans for additional public works will henceforth always be held ready, and applied more swiftly and effectively in any future recession. Incidentally, the argument that essential public works should not be postponed until such a time has validity; but there must always be some potentially useful forms of governmental spending that are only marginally desirable and which could therefore be introduced or stepped up in times of recession.

Finally, however little good a reduction in interest

rates might have proved to be in the recession, it could surely have done no harm—at any rate if it had been sharp and had therefore not been expected to be followed by a further reduction. The authorities seem to have had an exaggerated fear that a fall in interest rates, and consequently higher bond (and perhaps share) prices, might lead to a revival of the unhealthily speculative activity of 1960. But even if this had proved to be the case there would then still have been scope for raising interest rates again. In any case, keeping interest rates high in the recession left little scope for raising them if the long-expected boom had suddenly manifested itself.[2]

[2] H. W. Arndt and C. P. Harris suggest (*The Australian Trading Banks* (Melbourne, 1964), pp. 212–13) that 'Australian experience in 1961 and 1962 confirmed again that low interest rates can do little to stimulate business activity in the face of low business confidence'. But the argument of the foregoing section of the present study is that the minor reductions made in interest rates during this period were certainly not to 'low' levels; and, indeed, in real terms (i.e. allowing for changes in expectations about inflation) they were actually higher than in the 1960 boom. The present writer would argue that Australian experience during this period confirms that minor changes in officially controlled rates, lagging behind the market rates, are likely to be of little use—and perhaps even worse than useless.

1962 to 1963: Recovery and External Balance Leading to External Surplus

The February measures for economic expansion did not afford sufficient stimulus to bring a speedy return to full employment. Perhaps they showed most of their effects only after six months or so. If this is even a partial explanation, it stresses the need for corrective action to be taken as soon as possible, and further underlines the deficiencies of policy in 1961.

But despite the belated conversion to a reasonably expansionary budgetary policy, there remained an almost pathological aversion to the use of variations in interest rates (a reduction in which the Reserve Bank had according to its annual report very reasonably suggested to the government early in 1962). It is true, however, that in April 1962 fixed-interest-bearing deposit rates of banks were reduced—by ¼ per cent for the shorter maturities and by ½ per cent for the longer. But with the removal in April 1962 of the cumbersome and almost unworkable maximum imposed upon the *average* overdraft rates charged by banks, without any reduction being enforced in the *maximum* overdraft rate of banks, the average overdraft rate charged seems to have actually tended to rise. Those interest rates under official control were thus permitted to remain above their boom levels—even the nominal rates, still more the real level of interest rates (that is, allowing for the fact that over the intervening period inflationary expectations had given way to the experience and expectation of price stability).

But this hesitancy and half-heartedness about reducing bank interest rates were quite consistent with the Reserve Bank's policy of restraining the growth of new lending by the banks, which had risen fairly rapidly in 1961–2. As its 1963 report points out, new lending by the banks fell in the second half of 1962. This may have been partly a result of Reserve Bank policy and partly a consequence of the slowing down of the recovery of the economy.

As might have been expected, the investment allowances of February 1962 provided little incentive to industry to expand its investment in new capacity in a situation in which there was still ample capacity in most parts of the economy; though it is true that some gradual recovery in private investment took place in 1962–3.

The 1962 budget

In August 1962 it was clear that further stimulus was required if full employment was to be restored reasonably soon. The Treasurer clearly accepted this diagnosis and provided for considerable increases in expenditure, though the budget was probably less expansionary than that of August 1961 (which had been at the trough of the recession). But despite his emphasis on the government's determination to 'follow through with its expansionary programme until the economy is operating at the highest level of activity we can hope to sustain', the absence of any tax concession or increase in benefits did much to rule out any strong psychological effect from the budget—at a time when just such an impact on the outlook of the public was perhaps the prime requisite. An analysis of its probable effect on demand, relative to capacity, together with what might be expected of the other main sources of demand at the time, also suggested it was inadequate.[1] It is true that a sharp and sudden recovery of private investment might have proved the budget right in retrospect, and the policy-makers presumably thought that such a revival of demand could not be much longer delayed, and that the concessions on investment allowances announced in February 1962 might now at last have very sharp effects on business spending. One may grant that the nearer full employment approached, the more cautious the doses of expansion had to be, and that the over-caution that typified this budget was not as excessive as that which characterized policy in the previous year. But even if the Treasurer still feared a swift return of excess demand, one would have thought the wise course would still have been to reduce interest rates (now if not earlier), and thus to have in reserve the scope for a swift and sharp increase in them (pending anti-inflationary budgetary measures) if the budgetary stimulus had proved too

[1] In mentioning this view, which the author (*Economic Record*, August 1962) shared with many others, the intention is to place the budget in the context of thinking at the time. It is noteworthy that the surveys of the Australian economy published in the *Economic Record*, from that of Professor Bowen in 1960 until about 1963, generally suggested more forthright action—both in curbing the boom and in overcoming the recession—than the government saw fit to apply; and that in each case the academics happen to have been proved right in retrospect. On the other hand, it should be added that as full employment was more closely approached in 1963–4 the policy-makers were probably more nearly right than the academics—though, as we shall see, the budget of 1963 turned out to be right for the wrong reasons; and, in any case, the academics' doubts about its adequacy were much more cautiously phrased than had been their doubts about the previous budgets.

great. But the long-feared 'liquidity explosion' never occurred. Right up to the first half of 1964 the economy remained unwilling to use its high level of liquidity to support a level of spending such as a return to its 1960 habits would have made possible. The excessive caution of the reflationary measures appears to have been due to official fear that such a sharp revival of spending might occur.

The use made of interest-rate policy continued to be (as it had been ever since 1950) hesitant, reluctant and tardy. A reduction of interest rates was in fact made at last in March–April 1963 when it became clear (once again) that the budgetary stimulus had not been sufficient. It was then argued, very reasonably, that even if little additional stimulus to demand resulted from the reduction in interest rates, a reduction would afford scope for future increases if they became necessary. Though this argument was sound, and the change in interest rates welcome though belated, the reductions were of only ½ per cent on both maximum overdraft rates and fixed-interest-bearing deposit rates; and overdraft rates were in fact reduced on the average by only ¼ per cent. At this level, bank interest rates were still no lower than the levels prevailing right up to November 1960 in the worst of the boom; and in real terms (especially after two years of price stability) they were much higher.

Bond rates fell at last to a level appreciably below that prevailing during 1960; well into 1961 they had been allowed to remain at about the level to which they were raised late in 1960. By early 1963 they had come down, the long-term rate to 5 per cent; and by mid-1963 the long-term rate was reduced to about 4½ per cent.

This bears the appearance not of a conversion to a flexible interest-rate policy, but merely of a reluctant and partial acceptance of the need to modify—however slightly—the dogmatic rigidity of past interest-rate policies.

In February 1963 there were further measures to raise public authority expenditure, including finance for housing; housing finance also became more readily available from institutional sources at about this time. Building construction, especially that of dwellings (the low level of which had done much to intensify the recession), accordingly began to revive strongly in the second half of 1963. In any case, the building boom that followed was the main source of danger of excess demand, stimulated as it was by measures announced later to facilitate lending by savings banks, and by various government measures that would have been highly appropriate in 1961 or 1962, but which now served mainly to stimulate most the sector of the economy in which the danger of excess demand was already greatest.

Conclusions for future policy from the 1962–3 recovery

In 1962/3, as in 1961/2, official action to stimulate demand was too little and too late (but in the later period to a less blameworthy degree). The action that was taken was almost exclusively by way of budgetary measures (inadequate though even these proved to be), and the interest-rate weapon was not really employed until the recovery had slowly and hesitantly reached a point where the lagged effects of a reduction in interest rates—especially on building—might well come inconveniently late. Even then, the reductions made were only small. If the reduction in interest rates had been made sooner, any unwelcome upsurge in demand would have been easier to reverse (whether by budgetary or monetary measures). Moreover, an earlier reduction in official (especially bond) interest rates would have avoided the undesirable stimulus given to bond subscriptions from the public (by the natural expectation of rising bond prices and lower rates in future) which resulted from the delay in reducing bond rates. This was the opposite of the right policy at a time when the aim of the government should have been to divert funds from itself to the private sector.

It may seem odd that the interest-rate policy pursued in the recession was so markedly in conflict with what would seem to be sound policy for maintaining internal balance. A partial explanation was perhaps a fear on the part of the authorities that the high level of liquidity might suddenly be used to support an uncontainable rise in spending—far-fetched though this fear may now seem to have been at such a time of excess capacity.

But there may perhaps have been other arguments for avoiding the reduction in interest rates, based on certain official views about long-term debt policy. It may seem on the face of it strange to suggest that the Treasury (or the government generally) may have been reluctant to reduce interest rates in the recession, in view of the opposition which is generally believed to have been expressed in those quarters to a *rise* in interest rates in booms, because of a misplaced anxiety about the impact of this on tax needed to service the debt.[2] But it was apparently felt that one way of trying to reduce the long-term cost of servicing the national debt is to try to borrow relatively little when interest rates are high—in booms, and to borrow more when they are low—in

---

[2] 'Misplaced' because in fact higher interest rates in a boom help to restrain demand, and so make it possible to have lower tax rates (other things equal) than would otherwise be necessary to prevent excess demand.

recessions.[3] So far as this sort of consideration may influence debt policy it may inhibit the authorities from reducing bond (and other official) interest rates in recessions, since in any period when the expectation is that the next series of loans will be at a lower rate of interest (as was true for much of the period 1961–3) a Treasury will find that public subscriptions to loans come in at what it would presumably regard as an encouraging rate. But whatever may be said of such considerations in relation to the cost of servicing the debt, there is no doubt that their application must fly in the face of appropriate policy for securing internal balance. This does not necessarily mean that it would always be wrong to permit them to influence policy; but merely that if they are permitted to be decisive, the burden thus placed on other macro-economic measures will certainly be the greater. It must be wrong to permit such long-run considerations of the cost of servicing the debt to be decisive *unless* correspondingly stronger measures are taken to achieve the desired ends of macro-economic policy.

[3] Such an argument is especially difficult to sustain in respect of the period in question in view of the fact that bond rates were in 1962–3 actually as high as, or higher than, they had been in the previous boom in 1960 (up to November).

1963 to 1964: External Surplus and Full or Overfull Employment

The 1963 budget proved in retrospect to have afforded about the right amount of stimulus to the economy to bring it close to full employment by mid-1964. The minor sales-tax concessions and the increase in the minimum rate of income liable to tax in August 1963 were a minor influence raising demand. The major influence was the very sharp rise in government spending on goods and services and in its total outlay (including increases in some social services benefits and grants to states). Indeed, the combined effect of the tax concessions and the rise in outlay was to make this budget more expansionary than that of August 1962, although in 1963–4 the economy was much nearer to full employment.

Nevertheless, but for an unforeseeably high level of exports and capital inflow, and a remarkable continuance of the high level of spending on motor vehicles, it is doubtful whether such a high level of employment would have been achieved by mid-1964;[1] for it was presumably a sharp rise in private investment and consumption on which the government was counting most in deciding

---

[1] The Treasurer's reference to the rise in exports as having had 'a lot to do with' with the rise of 9 per cent in money G.N.P. (in his budget speech in 1964) might be read as an acknowledgment of this.

the general shape of its budget in 1963—yet these did not show sharp expansion until well into 1964.

Early in 1964 it became clear that if excess demand was to be avoided later in the year, measures would probably be required in the course of 1964 to restrain the rise in spending. For as full employment was progressively restored, nothing like the rapid rise in output achieved during the period of recovery could be expected. Yet the prospect was for rapid increases in most of the major forms of private and public spending, especially with the prospect of another sharp rise in money incomes following the basic wage judgment in the middle of the year—which was, as it turned out, at £1 a week (equivalent to $2) on the high side of the range of possibilities.[2]

In the first half of the year the principal anti-inflationary measures took the form of calls to S.R.D.s and increases in those interest rates under government influence and control. The period thus marked a milestone in Australian monetary policy, in that for the first time at a comparable period in an expansion, and in marked contrast to the policies of the three previous booms, anti-inflationary monetary measures including a rise in interest rates were applied. Bond and bank interest rates and the yield on Treasury Notes were increased, roughly in reversal of the reductions of a year earlier; and at the same time there were substantial sales of short-term bonds by the Reserve Bank. In addition, the trading banks were for the first time permitted to accept fixed-term deposits for one to three months, for large amounts, and also deposits for fifteen to twenty-

[2] Two of the members of the commission gave their judgment for 10s and two for £1, the president giving his casting vote for the latter alternative.

four months from October 1964. The limits on the portfolios of the official money-market firms were removed in the middle of the year. These various measures must have had some effect in curbing any tendency for the share market to rise and in making it harder for non-bank intermediaries and firms borrowing in the inter-company loan market to compete for funds with the banks, with the Treasury (by way of bond subscriptions and purchases of Treasury Notes), and with the official money-market.

The calls to S.R.D.s did little more than offset part of the big rise in bank liquidity resulting from the balance of payments surplus. The opposition to some of the calls early in 1964 on the part of certain spokesmen for the trading banks therefore appears to have been misplaced. The banks still remained very liquid and unused overdrafts considerable. Had the central bank not felt it wise to take account of the feelings of private trading bankers, it might perhaps have preferred in such a situation to keep the banks more firmly against their agreed minimum L.G.S. ratios by still greater calls to S.R.D.s—especially in the light of its difficulties in restraining bank lending in earlier booms. (It must, however, be remembered that the L.G.S. ratio was not statutory, and that if too great a pressure had been placed upon the private trading banks by calls to S.R.D.s it might have led some of the banks to allow their L.G.S. ratio to lapse below this agreed minimum.)

By August 1964 the general level of activity was near to full employment—and approaching it more closely, at least if one looks at the crucial evidence of the state of the labour market, especially that for skilled labour. It is true, however, that there was spare capacity in some industries and only the building industry (among the main forms of activity) appeared in serious danger of over-strain. The balance of payments remained very strong with reserves at a record level.

The main problem facing the Treasurer in August 1964 was thus to ensure that total demand in the coming year rose in step with the rise in capacity (plus whatever rise in imports might occur) but no faster than this. The rise in the basic wage and its repercussions on money incomes was bound to bring a considerable rise in consumption, and the government stood committed to much higher grants to the states (partly to offset the effect on their budgets of the wage increases) and to a sharp rise in defence spending, as well as to the normal 'built-in' increases in spending associated with rising population. Moreover, there was evidence that private investment—which apart from that in building had been rising less strongly than had been expected when the previous budget was presented—was beginning to advance more confidently, and spending on vehicles showed no clear sign of slackening, whilst that on building continued to rise rapidly. On the other hand, a very large additon to the work force (both from juveniles leaving school and higher immigration) was expected during 1964–5, and ample international reserves existed to permit a considerable rise in imports. Supplies would therefore be available to meet a considerable rise in total demand, perhaps of the order of 5½ per cent to 6 per cent (at constant prices) over the year, even though nothing like the recovery rates of growth of output of the previous year or two could be expected.

Moreover, for the first time at any comparable stage of the cycle the Treasurer could frame his budget in the knowledge that monetary measures, including the essential element of interest-rate policy, would be working to reinforce any budgetary measures he adopted to restrain demand. The rise in interest rates earlier in the year had, indeed, been followed by a further rise in bond rates just before the budget (the long-term rate rising to 5 per cent).

The principal anti-inflationary measures in the budget were: the repeal of the '5 per cent rebate' on personal income tax; a rise of 6d in the pound on company tax; a rise of 2½ per cent in sales-tax on cars; an increase in excise on tobacco, and certain increases in telephone charges. In sum, the rise in tax receipts was apparently intended to offset (or even more than offset) the further sharp rise in government outlay. Although most of these tax increases had been widely discussed before the event, their wide range was slightly surprising—though it is true that a rise in petrol tax, another widely mooted measure, was not included.

This budget seemed to confirm the place of the '5 per cent rebate' as the main anti-cyclical budgetary weapon; for it had now been granted and removed with each change of the cycle since it was originally granted in 1959. Rescinded in August 1960 (as an anti-inflationary measure), revived (belatedly) in early 1962 to stimulate demand, its removal was now again to be used to perform a key role in restraining the rise in demand at full employment. The fact that these effective changes in income-tax rates were never fully incorporated into the tax schedules may have made it psychologically easier to reimpose or remove the rebate.[3] But it is likely that a

[3] The income-tax payer, filling in his assessment form and making his own estimate of tax liability, was in every year given the same table from which to calculate his tax. In the years when the rebate operated he had then in making his final assessment simply to subtract 5 per cent from his 'tax liability' so calculated. This may have served to underline the temporary, anti-cyclical nature of the rebate and thus to make its removal psychologically more acceptable. This consideration—and that of simplicity—might be set against the probably more equitable and effective alternative of frequent revision of the whole income-tax structure to secure a given effect on disposable incomes allocated in whatever way might be thought to accord best with all criteria, including those of social desirability.

change in income-tax rates will have more effect on the taxpayer's consumption if he does *not* expect the change in rates to be temporary.

The spreading of the increases over a fairly wide range of direct and indirect taxation gave at least the appearance of being 'equitable', and was probably in this sense appropriate for curbing a generalized rise in demand at or near full employment. But though there were particular areas of the economy where the danger of excess demand was considerable, there was also a range of industries in which there was more adequate capacity. The rise of 2½ per cent in the sales-tax on cars was presumably intended partly to restrain demand in one area of demand where spending was likely to rise well above the long-run trend (and so the desirable long-run capacity of the industry). But no special budgetary measures were directed at restraining the rise in spending on dwelling construction. Indeed the implementation of the government's election promise of a £250 subsidy to certain categories of house purchasers with approved classes of savings was one factor helping to swell the demand for dwellings to a point where building costs and prices of finished houses were increasing sharply. It was suggested that measures directed towards keeping the pressure of demand on the resources of the building industry down nearer its physical capacity might have made it less necessary to take more general anti-inflationary measures on such a considerable scale. The monetary authorities were in the position of having to try to offset, by the limited means at their disposal—curtailment of the rate of new lending by the Commonwealth Savings Bank, and requests to other savings banks to do likewise—the effect of the budgetary measures that stimulated (rather than restrained) dwelling construction. It has also been suggested that one purpose of permitting the trading banks to accept 15- to 24-month deposits (as from October 1964) was to enable them to attract some deposits from the savings banks, and so reduce the resources available to the latter, which were among the principal suppliers of housing finance. These measures seem to have had some success in reducing the strain on the building industry by the end of 1964.

The measures of domestic policy taken in 1964 indicated that—in contrast to each of the previous postwar booms—the policy-makers had apparently accepted that it was both possible and useful to operate interest-rate policy in harmony with budgetary policy, as well as with quantitative controls over bank lending. The weight placed upon each of these other instruments of policy was consequently less, and proper use was made of the rate of interest as a weapon of policy that could readily and quickly be varied (in contrast to most budgetary measures and also in contrast to the level of bank lending). At the same time the general rise in official and bank interest rates probably did not fully offset the upward revision of expectations about the price level that must have been occurring during 1964. But the authorities seem on this occasion to have appreciated that early action is desirable before full employment is reached (provided that the forces of expansion are strongly upwards), for the effects of anti-inflationary measures are likely to take some months to show themselves. By contrast, in previous periods of expansion the failure to apply adequate anti-inflationary measures (especially a rise in interest rates) early in the upswing had agravated the problems of dealing with excess demand. This criticism could certainly not be levelled at monetary policy in 1964. Both the timing and the nature of the measures seem to have been appropriate in the first half of the year; and the total anti-inflationary impact of the budgetary and monetary measures of 1964 was sufficient to prevent appreciable excess demand arising in 1965.

The external surplus, 1963–4

For the first time since the Korean War, Australia experienced during this period a state of balance of payments surplus combined with full (or nearly full) employment. In this context the term 'balance of payments surplus' is to be interpreted as meaning not merely that the country was adding to its international reserves (as it was), but that it had been doing so to such an extent that there was a strong case for taking corrective action of some sort to reduce the country's reserves.

After a decade in white balance of payments difficulties had been almost continually present, it was perhaps not surprising that the government and commentators on the economic scene should have given remarkably little public recognition to this changed state of affairs. The strength of the balance of payments was naturally often remarked upon, but in terms that failed to recognize that an unnecessarily strong balance of payments is as much a failure of policy as an unnecessarily weak one.[4] For the aim of balance of payments policy must be to use the country's external receipts in such a way that over a period of years they may make the maximum contribution to economic growth (principally that of Australia, but in some sense, perhaps, that of the whole of the world). Just as it slows down a country's economic growth to have periods when its

---

[4] By a sort of reflex action (born of years of balance of payments anxieties) some newspapers were inclined to be somewhat worried about the rise in imports in mid-1964, although in the circumstances it was in fact to be thoroughly welcomed.

reserves are so low that it has to curtail imports (by import controls or deflation), in the same way it is also a failure of its policy if it does not use its available foreign exchange to buy the imports that would help it to maximize its rate of economic growth (over good and bad years together). An adequate balance of payments policy will see that these conflicting considerations are held in proper balance. The aim should be to see that reserves are built up in good times just sufficiently to meet the requirements of the bad years that can reasonably be expected, bearing in mind the other liquid resources (especially I.M.F. drawing rights) that may be available to the country. But beyond a certain point, the extra insurance against future contingencies afforded by a rise in reserves is obviously not worth the immediate sacrifice of useful imported goods that it involves. It should, in particular, be borne in mind that the higher rate of economic growth in the immediate future resulting from a higher level of imports may also contribute towards making the economy better able to withstand possible future reductions in its external receipts. To that extent, using reserves now may actually be as helpful as building them up against a rainy day.

It is true that the period under discussion was one when there was a quite unusual number of presumably temporary favourable influences upon the Australian balance of payments; so that it could be argued that it was appropriate to take advantage of them to rebuild the reserves for possible use in years when these influences might be equally unfavourable. Nevertheless, it could reasonably be asked whether the reserves were not being built up unnecessarily high—bearing in mind the sacrifice of useful imports that this involved, and the considerable 'second-line reserves' of I.M.F. drawing rights, including the new provision to permit an extra 25 per cent of a primary-exporting country's quota to be available to it in the event of an unforeseeable fall in its export receipts (which went almost completely unpublicized in Australia, though it is a very relevant consideration for appraising whether the reserves were being permitted to rise excessively high).

Viewing the matter from a slightly wider point of view, it could reasonably be argued that if the other countries of the world aimed at building up reserves as high in good years as did Australia in this period (relative to their annual requirements of foreign exchange) the outlook for world trade—and not least for Australia as an important trading country—would be very adversely affected. Some readiness to avoid an over-cautious policy in good years would strengthen Australia's hand in asking others to pursue policies likely to maintain a high rate of growth of world trade in other circumstances. More immediately, the urgent requirements of many underdeveloped countries for foreign exchange were such that they could certainly not indulge in the luxury of accumulating reserves. If an appropriate emphasis had been placed on Australia's interests in doing what she could to facilitate world economic growth, some part of her high reserves could well have been devoted to increasing aid to underdeveloped countries and increasing her imports from them.

If the writer might state his preference among the various measures that could be applied in any period of unnecessarily high reserves, it would be: (a) increase aid to underdeveloped countries and stimulate Australian investment in them; (b) reduce those tariffs or other limitations on imports that have the greatest degree of protective effect (unless very strong grounds exist for maintaining them), especially on the products that underdeveloped countries can most readily export to us. But a temporary subsidy on some or all imports or an appreciation should not be ruled out from consideration.

1965 to 1966: Mild Recession with External Balance

During the course of 1965/6 the economy moved from a state of close to full employment into a situation where there was considerable spare capacity and the level of unemployment was tending to rise. At the same time, the balance of payments remained reasonably strong.

One reason for the slowing down of demand was a drought in some areas and a consequent check to rural expenditure. There had been a decline in exports in 1964/5 mainly as a result of falls in certain export prices, and its effects were being felt by 1965. Another factor was that private fixed capital expenditure rose very much less rapidly in 1965/6 after several years in which it had grown especially rapidly and had thus led to the existence of a good deal of spare capacity in a number of industries.

At the time of the budget in August 1965, however, the main concern of the government was still the prevention of excess demand, especially in view of the very sharp rise in its defence expenditure that it was planning. But much of the defence expenditure was taking place overseas (perhaps more than was at first allowed for) and the part of it that took place within Australia may have taken longer to work its way through to incomes than the government expected.

The fear that a new burst of excess demand might

result led the government to introduce a number of tax increases, including a 2½ per cent surcharge on personal income tax. This represented a further refinement of the anti-cyclical impositions and removals of a surcharge (hitherto of 5 per cent) or a rebate. In retrospect, it would probably have been preferable to offer a *rebate* of this order, rather than a *surcharge*. For the tax increases and some rises in public utility charges clawed back a large part of the wage increases that occurred in 1966. There seems also to have been some increase in the willingness of people to save—which may well have been associated with the return of virtual price stability after several years of inflation.

There were some measures directed at sustaining demand, especially the provision of some drought relief, and a gradual easing of the tight control over bank lending, which prevailed up to 1965—initially for loans to drought-affected areas and then for housing (expenditure on which fell sharply in 1965). The Commonwealth government also made supplementary allocations of funds to the states under the Commonwealth and States Housing Agreement. But no reduction was made during the year in those interest rates under government control, though this might have afforded a worthwhile stimulus.

Perhaps the government felt that the creation of some slack in the economy was defensible, in order to facilitate the necessary transfer of resources to the expanding defence sector and towards the mineral developments (in the west especially). Nevertheless, the lapse from full employment presumably went rather further than the government intended, even though unemployment during 1965/6 never rose even as high as in 1963/4 and was thus far below that of 1961/2 and 1962/3.

On the side of the balance of payments, there was some anxiety in 1965, despite the high level of the reserves, for there was a sharp fall in them during 1964–5. The continued high level of imports and the prospect of reduced earnings from exports as a result of the drought gave cause for some anxiety, and in both years there was a reasonable expectation of a fall in capital outflow from Britain and the United States, partly as a result of policy measures taken by the governments of these countries. In particular, in March 1966 Britain imposed 'voluntary' control over the flow of certain types of capital to Australia (and certain other countries that had previously had free access to British capital). Nevertheless, Australia's international reserves were high, and rose slightly in 1965–6, largely because capital inflow continued at a record level.[1] Anxieties about the balance of payments could, therefore, be based only upon the fear that some of the favourable influences upon the balance of payments during the period might prove temporary. One of these was the very large inflow of capital to finance initial stages of the mineral developments in Western Australia. Another was the check to imports that resulted from the very cautious attitudes in business during 1966.

[1] The flow of capital from Britain was temporarily stimulated by the controls announced in March 1966—as firms hastened to bring out capital before the restraint became fully effective.

1967 to 1970: Recovery to Full Employment with External Balance

During the years 1967–70 the Australian economy recovered from operating at rather less than its capacity up to full, or perhaps even overfull, employment. For by 1969 the problem had become one of seeing that serious excess demand did not arise. There was, however, no serious concern over the balance of payments, for capital inflow and the growth of exports continued to offset the rising level of imports, including government overseas spending on defence. Nevertheless, as we shall see, a consideration of the possible effects of macro-economic policies upon capital inflow does seem to have played some part in determining the measures taken; though such considerations were probably not dominant, and in any case probably did not lead to the adoption of measures that were undesirable from other points of view.

The peak level of unemployment (on a seasonally adjusted basis) was reached during the second half of 1967; but the lapse from full capacity operation of the economy in 1966/7 was heavily concentrated upon farm output; non-farm output fell only slightly below its trend. Nevertheless, non-farm output rose slightly faster than in 1965/6, whilst farm output rose still more sharply by comparison with 1965/6. Unemployment fell during 1968/9, whilst unfilled vacancies rose, but full employment was not completely restored until 1969/70. In that year the principal aim of policy was to prevent demand rising so high as to cause excess demand and serious price rises, whilst ensuring that any anti-inflationary measures taken were not so strong as to precipitate another recession.

Over the course of this period the budget was used with some success to offset the fluctuations in other sources of demand; for total domestic outlay provided for in the Commonwealth budget rose at an appreciably faster rate in 1966/7 than in the previous year, whilst the rate of increase in tax receipts was less than the rise in the value of output. It is true, however, that the expansionary influence exerted through the budget was insufficient to prevent a rise in unemployment during 1966/7 and a fall in the extent of utilization of the country's economic capacity; but the principal weapons were varied in the appropriate direction—if on an insufficient scale (as can be seen in retrospect). Perhaps the removal of the 2½ per cent levy on personal income tax imposed in 1965, or even its replacement by a rebate of 2½ per cent or 5 per cent (or some comparable reduction in taxation) would have been worth-while. It is certainly worth noting that this was the first clear case since the first rebate (of 5 per cent) on personal income tax in 1959 when the state of activity had moved into a markedly different phase without a levy being imposed or removed, or a rebate granted, on personal income tax.

Presumably the need for a stimulus to demand was underestimated by the government partly because of the rapid rise that was occurring in demand. For 1966–7 saw a rise in G.N.P. at current prices of the order of 10 per cent, and a rise in real G.N.P. at well above trend rates, with very little inflation. Nevertheless, the economy was clearly working at below capacity in that year, and at an above average level of unemployment, presumably because the rapid rise in investment in previous years had greatly increased its capacity, and because the recovery of farm output from the previous drought did relatively little to increase employment, of city workers at any rate. The view that the earlier sharp rises in private fixed investment—to a very high peak in 1964/5 and 1965/6—had greatly increased the capacity of the economy is to some extent borne out by the fact that private fixed capital investment rose very little in 1966/7, in the face of a strongly rising level of overall demand.

Despite the spare capacity and the absence of any strong stimulus from tax concessions during 1966–8, the authorities did not permit any considerable reductions in those interest rates under official control. Maximum overdraft rates and rates on the savings banks' housing loans to individuals remained at the peak levels that had prevailed in 1964/5 and 1965/6, though there were small reductions in certain bond rates and in the rates payable on the shorter-term fixed deposits with trading banks. If one makes allowance—as one should—for the fact that the extent of inflation was much less in 1966/7 than in 1964/5 or 1965/6, this meant that *real* interest rates were appreciably higher than in the previous boom (that is, if one adjusts nominal rates for peoples' expectations about the probable rate of inflation, using as a rough indication of these expectations the rise in prices that was being experienced at the time). We have seen that in the recession of 1961/2 also real interest rates were lower than those prevailing in the boom of 1960. Despite that earlier experience, therefore, the policy-makers' habit of thinking in terms of nominal rather than real interest rates when determining policy was apparently dying very hard.

One consideration that probably carried weight with

the authorities was that interest rates in a number of overseas countries were higher than the corresponding rates in Australia. Further reduction in overdraft rates and bond rates (for example) in Australia would have widened this differential; and perhaps this would have adversely affected net capital inflow, especially by making the Australian branches and subsidiaries of overseas companies more likely to borrow within Australia and therefore less likely to bring in capital from overseas. The decision not to reduce appreciably those interest rates under official influence may thus have been prompted by this view, coupled with fears that the prevailing British and American policies to limit capital outflow might adversely affect those countries' investment in Australia. For the strength of Australia's external balance had come to depend to a considerable extent on the maintenance of something like the recent rate of capital inflow. Given the unwillingness to use the exchange rate, such variations of the combination of monetary and budgetary measures, with a view to reconciling internal and external balance, may well be defensible. But if interest rates were not to be reduced in this situation, the proper use of these weapons at that time would have involved a much more expansionary use of the budget to offset the depressing domestic effects of not allowing the level of interest rates within Australia to fall. It ought not, therefore, to have been surprising that with real interest rates probably higher than at any time since the 1961—2 recession, private investment lagged appreciably as the economy recovered. In addition, other factors, notably the high level of investment that had prevailed up to 1965, also played their part in reducing the incentive to install new capacity.

The crux of the matter was really that the reconciliation of internal and external balance by merely varying the combination and the overall effect of budgetary and monetary measures is often likely to be impossible. Certainly if one also includes other objectives—such as keeping interest rates at the right level to secure an appropriate stimulus to investment or to capital inflow—some other weapon is likely to be required.

In principle this weapon is ready to hand in the exchange rate. But the Australian authorities continued to be unwilling to vary the exchange rate even when the devaluation of sterling in November 1967 presented an occasion when this could have been done with considerable ease.

It is true, however, that the strength of the balance of payments at the time made it difficult to justify devaluation on external grounds, even though the actual level of Australia's reserves was not—in relation to imports—appreciably stronger than in some periods of serious balance of payments difficulty in the past; for the outlook for the balance of payments was good. Another good argument for not devaluing on this occasion was that the maximum assistance could be given to Britain if as many countries as possible refrained from devaluing with her.

Whatever the arguments for and against devaluation in November 1967 from the viewpoint of the balance of payments, one argument used by the Treasurer at the time—to the effect that it would have been undesirably inflationary—seems in retrospect to be the reverse of the truth. It would in fact have provided a very desirable degree of stimulus to the economy, which remained less than fully employed throughout 1967/8, even if such a decision might have increased the need for more restraining measures in the subsequent year.

During the course of 1967/8 the recorded rise in real

G.N.P. was less than the trend, because farm output fell sharply owing to the effects of another drought—with non-farm output rising at above the trend rate of increase. But, partly under the impact of the drought, unemployment still continued at or near its peak levels right through 1967/8, whilst unfilled vacancies still showed no clear tendency to rise. Again, therefore, one may conclude that the total effect of monetary and budgetary policy was insufficiently expansionary, but—as in 1965/6 and its aftermath—the onset of drought and its indirect effects were probably at least partly responsible for the failure to maintain something closer to full capacity operation.

The rise in domestic outlay in the Commonwealth budget played an important part in bringing about the gradual recovery in non-farm output; for this rise in government outlay was appreciably above trend, though by no means as large as in 1966/7. Tax receipts rose considerably faster than did G.N.P. (at current prices) because of the inbuilt progressivity of the tax system, which thus acted as a 'fiscal drag' on the level of demand; so that there was, in effect, an (unannounced) rise in tax rates (in relation to incomes). This offset to a considerable extent the stimulus given by the rise in government outlay.

Nor was interest-rate policy used to afford any additional stimulus, for those interest rates under direct control of the authorities were maintained at virtually the same levels as during the preceding three years, and there was even some tendency for some government bond rates to edge upwards in the second half of 1967/8.

During the course of 1967/8 private fixed capital investment started to revive, and by the end of 1967/8 it was rising at a rate above its long-run trend. But exports were weak (largely as a result of the drought), so that it was the sustained rise in private consumption and in government spending that together provided the main impetus for the revival of the economy towards full employment.

During 1968/9 the economy recovered very nearly to full employment, with private and public fixed capital expenditure now leading the way, together with a recovery of exports as the worst effects of the drought passed away and as minerals and manufactures became exports of rapidly increasing importance. With both farm and non-farm output rising strongly, a rise in real G.N.P. of some 9 per cent was achieved, and by the end of 1968/9 unemployment had fallen below its average level (in relation to the work force), whilst overtime worked was rising sharply.

In order to restrain the rise in demand resulting from the combined effect of another considerable increase in government outlay (though at a lower rate than in the two preceding years) and of the rising demand from consumption, together with the resumed growth of private investment, the government decided to make certain increases in tax rates in the budget of 1968. These were a rise of 2½ cents in the dollar on company taxation and an increase in the general rate of sales-tax from 12½ to 13 per cent (on a range of goods including commercial vehicles and motor spare parts and accessories, but not private vehicles). The expected effect of these measures was to increase revenue by about $100m (or about 2 per cent). In addition, without any announced rise in the rates of personal income taxation, receipts from pay-as-you-earn income tax rose by as much as 15 per cent, whilst G.N.P. at current prices rose by about 12½ per cent. The inbuilt progressivity of the pay-as-you-earn income tax, which had acted as a drag on recovery during 1967/8, thus helped to prevent excess demand from emerging as higher levels of activity were established in 1968/9.

These budgetary measures were reinforced by an appropriate use of monetary policy, with the maximum bank overdraft rate and the rates on savings banks' loans for housing being raised during the year, as well as the rates on government securities. Bank fixed-interest-bearing deposit rates had been increased slightly towards the end of 1967/8 and were not further increased during 1968/9, but there was a rise in savings bank deposit rates during the year.

In sum, during 1968/9 both budgetary and monetary measures contributed towards bringing about a return to full employment without any serious increase in the extent of inflation.

During 1969/70 unemployment continued at a low level, and there was some anxiety on the part of the government that serious excess demand might arise; unfilled vacancies continued to fall, and there was some tendency for prices to rise more rapidly than previously. But in general the budget was again well calculated to maintain full employment without allowing the economy to lapse into serious excess demand or into recession. The rise in the Commonwealth government's domestic outlays was considerably less than in the three previous years, and tax receipts (both in total and those from pay-as-you-earn income tax) rose very much more sharply (by about 15 per cent) than did G.N.P. at current prices (which showed a rise of just over 10 per cent). The built-in progressivity of the tax structure was thus again an important element in restraining demand from rising too high at full employment.

Nevertheless, the government became somewhat concerned during the course of 1969/70 that demand might be rising too high. A succession of monetary measures was therefore taken during the course of the year, partly to curb the rise in demand, and apparently also in order to help maintain the level of net capital inflow, which showed signs of flagging about the middle of the year 1969/70. Long-term bond rate was increased from 5½ to 6 per cent early in 1969/70 (in the face of high and rising rates in other countries); bank interest rates were also raised in the first half of the financial year—by ¼ per cent all round, except that savings banks rates remained unchanged.

But it was not until the second half of the financial year (in March 1970) that a really tight monetary policy was enforced, by open-market operations and further sharp rises in officially controlled interest rates (bond rates by another 1 per cent, trading bank interest rates by about ¼ to ½ per cent). The rates on savings banks' loans to individuals for housing were increased very sharply, from 5½ to 6¼ per cent, and at the same time the savings banks were permitted to offer more attractive terms to depositors, especially for large deposits.

One effect of these moves, together with some rise in the banks' Statutory Reserve Deposit ratio during the year, was that the very rapid rise in dwelling construction, which had been one of the principal expansionary forces in the rapid rise in demand during 1969/70, was sharply curbed; partly because the building societies (especially in New South Wales and Western Australia), which had provided a large part of the finance for the rise in dwelling construction, were faced by sharp withdrawals of their deposits as a result of more attractive rates of interest now being offered elsewhere (especially by savings banks); whilst the much higher rates of interest charged by the savings banks, the most important lenders for housing, also may have reduced the demand for housing. Apparently neither the building societies nor the savings banks (in those cases where the latter held more bonds than the minimum that they were required to hold) were willing to sell bonds on a substantial scale in order to increase their loans for housing; for this would have meant sustaining a considerable loss on the market value of these bonds, in view of the recent sharp falls in bond prices. These holders were thus, in effect, 'locked in' to their bond holdings, at any rate temporarily. It seems that the very abrupt curtailment of housing finance and the downturn in building approvals towards the end of 1969/70 caused the authorities some concern; for near the end of the 1969/70 year both trading banks and savings banks were encouraged by the Reserve Bank to lend more freely for housing. Presumably if the savings banks found themselves with more than the maximum permitted ratio of loans for housing to total deposits, as a result of conforming to the central bank's request to lend more freely for housing, they had some reason to believe that the authorities would vary appropriately this control that limited the proportion of loans for housing to their total assets (which was done later in the year). In any event, a sharp revival of bank lending for housing occurred in July 1970, thus alleviating the weakness of one of the principal sources of demand that had slackened sharply during the preceding months.

The overall effect of macro-economic measures during the course of 1969/70 was probably about right, at least if one was prepared to tolerate some temporary increase in the extent of inflation. Apparently the official view at the time of the 1970 budget was that it was both possible and desirable to keep the economy at about the prevailing level in relation to capacity during 1970/1. The overall effect on demand of the tax changes—income tax rates down, a wide range of indirect tax rates and company tax rates up—was apparently intended to be small. There was almost certainly a reduction in the extent of the progressivity of the whole tax structure (compared with its structure if no changes in income tax rates and indirect taxes had been made), but the expected rise in total tax receipts over the year was rather more than the likely rise in G.N.P. at current prices. But the government's domestic outlay was expected to rise rather more than this—and also by more than it had in 1969/70. If this was not to result in excess demand, this implied that the government was expecting some slowing down in the rate of growth in other sources of demand. In fact, about the middle of 1970 there were some indications that the peak level of activity had passed.

Before the end of 1970, however, the labour market had tightened again at about the level of full employment (as normally understood in Australia), and prices and money incomes were apparently rising more rapidly than for many years. It is true that the rise in indirect taxation in the budget was partly responsible for the sharp rise in the consumer price index in the December quarter; but, quite apart from this, prices were apparently beginning to rise more rapidly—as, indeed, they were in nearly every country, even where considerably less than full employment (especially by Australian standards) prevailed. In November the Arbitration Commission awarded an increase of 6 per cent in the total wage—in the wake of rapid rises in many other incomes.

The government was increasingly concerned at the evidence of increasing inflation and early in 1971 it withdrew the investment allowances to manufacturing industry (originally granted in 1962) and curbed the rate of increase in Commonwealth government spending (and indirectly that of the states). These measures were certainly defensible in terms of their macro-economic effects (however debatable some of the downward effects on desirable forms of outlay may have been). But there remained some doubt whether there was a real threat of serious excess demand; it seemed more likely that—even at full, but not overfull, employment—prices and money incomes were tending to rise more rapidly than in the past. This would suggest that the appropriate remedy would be direct measures of some sort to reduce inflation from the cost side (by some form of prices and incomes policy, if this proved feasible). For unless some such measures could be successfully applied it might be difficult to keep unemployment down to the satisfactorily low levels generally achieved in the later 1960s without suffering the inequities and inefficiencies of accelerating inflation.

1971 to 1972: Stagflation with External Surplus

The slackening in the rate of activity that had appeared during the second half of 1970 became increasingly apparent in the course of 1971. But the official attitude continued to be one of restraint, exemplified by the withdrawal in February 1971 of the investment allowance and by a continued tightness of monetary policy. The ending of the mining boom was an important influence changing the business outlook from expansion to recession; and another important factor was an increasingly cautious attitude on the part of consumers, leading them to save a higher proportion of their disposable incomes.

Sharply rising wage rates and higher prices for imports both contributed to bringing about a marked rise in the rate of inflation. Higher unit costs in manufacturing industry, as capacity became less fully employed, also contributed to cost-inflation. As the external account was strong, the appropriate external policy would have been to ensure, by an appropriate exchange rate and tariff policy, that this external strength was used to increase the availability of imports, as a means of restraining price increases within Australia, whilst ensuring that budgetary and monetary policy was expansionary enough to absorb the extra imports without a lapse below full employment.

The actual policy adopted, however, failed to do this. The balance of payments and the level of the reserves were allowed to remain excessively strong, whilst the level of activity was allowed to fall well below full employment by the taking of measures directed against demand inflation, whereas it was primarily cost-inflation that was now the real problem. In particular, the budget of 1971 was a serious mistake in the deflationary direction and the higher tax rates included in it themselves contributed to wage and cost inflation. Most observers saw the budget at the time as being too deflationary, and government leaders and their advisers apparently came round to this view not long after the budget. It could perhaps be defended on the grounds that the rapid rise in disposable incomes that had been occurring might reasonably, on past precedent, have led to a much faster rise in consumption than in fact occurred. Alternatively, one could defend it on the grounds that if it led to some rise in unemployment this might, on the basis of past experience, be expected to reduce considerably the rate of inflation, which was now becoming dangerously high.

But Australia—in common with most other countries—was now experiencing the new phenomenon of 'stagflation', that is, a combination of stagnation (or actual decline) and inflation, a tendency for the price level to rise uncomfortably rapidly at less than full employment. This meant that, unless a country was prepared to tolerate very much higher levels of unemployment than had been known in the period since World War II, the conventional policy reaction to inflation, by way of higher tax rates and restraint in government spending, was not likely to arrest the inflation and would make the unemployment worse. Instead of substantially increasing its outlay on goods and services the government budgeted in August 1971 for only a very small rise in the money value of its capital expenditure, which represented a fall in real terms in this major item. Moreover, it increased both income-tax rates and a range of indirect-tax rates (including that on petrol, which appreciably affects a wide range of costs, as well as the consumer price index). On the budgetary side, then, some of the main measures adopted were the exact reverse of what was required.

The official expectation at the time of the budget seems to have been for a strong rise in consumption in response to the rapid rise in money incomes that had been occurring. But there was instead a sharp rise (unparalleled in previous periods with a similar level of unemployment) in the proportion of their incomes that people decided to save. Various factors may have contributed to this, but the main one was presumably the general uncertainty that people felt in a situation where relatively high and rising unemployment was occurring at the same time as unusually rapid inflation. This presumably led many of them to devote a high proportion of their current earnings to building up a 'nest-egg'.

Before long the policy-makers began to realize the extent to which their assumptions about the state of the economy had been mistaken; but there appears to have been some reluctance on their part to admit so soon and so openly by taking new budgetary measures that the assumptions on which the budget of August 1971 had been based were wrong. This delay presumably lengthened and deepened the subsequent recession, though an easing of monetary policy began in October. But in December 1971 and February 1972 steps were taken to increase Commonwealth allocations to the states for certain purposes including the relief of nonmetropolitan unemployment, which was especially high. In February, too, some direct stimulus to the business sector was provided by re-introducing investment allowances on manufacturing plant and equipment, and substantial increases were made in unemployment benefits. But no steps were taken to reverse the increase in a number of indirect taxes that had been made in August 1971, though these clearly added to cost-push inflation.

It might also have been argued that the rising effective rates of income tax that resulted as people moved into higher income tax brackets, partly as a result of the sharp increase in the rate of inflation, may have been beginning to affect some wage and salary demands (as people tried to maintain their post-tax incomes in the face of these higher tax rates). So far as this may have been true, the belated reduction (in April 1972) from 5 to 2½ per cent in the levy on personal income tax was especially to be welcomed, for even if its expansionary effect was belated it should at least have had some tendency to reduce wage-push inflation. These expansionary measures were not taken early enough, however, to prevent a substantial rise in unemployment to recession levels during 1972.

Meanwhile, prices and money incomes continued to rise fairly rapidly, partly in consequence of Arbitration Commission judgments in 1970 and 1971. Despite the higher level of unemployment money wage rates continued to rise at an unusually rapid rate. Sharply rising import prices up to mid-1972 contributed to higher prices within Australia, and a boom in export prices, especially from late 1972, also helped to transfer inflation from the outside world into Australia.

The appropriate remedy for this rise in the prices of internationally traded goods generally—an appreciation—was not, however, taken up by the Liberal-Country Party government, largely because of the political power of the Country Party partner, which successfully resisted pressure to appreciate the currency to a more appropriate level when there was a general realignment of the exchange rates of various countries at the end of 1971.

The balance of payments situation and the level of international reserves in 1972 were certainly such as would have justified appreciation of the Australian dollar. Exports were strong, imports depressed and capital inflow was high; whilst the reserves had benefited from about two years of very low imports. It is true that part of the capital inflow was temporary and speculative, as a result of the widespread view that an appreciation of the Australian dollar was likely, and to that extent the foreign exchange it brought could not reasonably have been used to buy more imports. But until the required exchange rate alteration was made, one could not know how much of the capital inflow was in this category. This obvious undervaluation of the Australian dollar was an open invitation to overseas investors to build up their holdings of Australian dollars, and for Australians to defer overseas payments as long as possible, in the expectation that an upward revaluation must occur before long. So far as this capital inflow was reversed when the revaluation eventually occurred, it was bound to involve Australia in a real cost in terms of foreign exchange (as the foreign exchange paid out after an appreciation would exceed that which had been received when the capital inflow came in).

The only excuse for not revaluing that was even superficially plausible was the adverse effect that such an action, if taken alone, would have had on the level of employment in Australia. But no one could reasonably have advocated an appropriate adjustment of the exchange rate without also advocating appropriate budgetary or monetary measures of expansion sufficient to see that the level of activity was not adversely affected. Of course, the spokesmen for various vested interests, especially rural producers and mining, were opposed to the idea of revaluation as likely to reduce their share in national income, but the appropriate way of avoiding any undesired consequences for them (if such a course were considered politically necessary) would have been by way of extra subsidies or tax concessions. These could have been introduced as part of the expansionary budgetary measures that would have been needed to offset and avoid the depressing internal effects of an appreciation. This would have been a far less damaging way of buying their support than inflicting on the country the inflation and the reduction in living standards that resulted from the undervaluation of the Australian dollar in 1972.

Policy in 1972

Even before expansionary measures were undertaken to reverse the deflationary effects of the budget of August 1971, monetary measures of expansion were begun (from October 1971), thus relaxing the fairly tight rein on which monetary policy had been held with the expansion of the money supply restrained throughout the financial year 1970–1. The rising rate of capital inflow during the latter part of 1971, and then increasingly in 1972, also helped to bring about a very sharp expansion of the money supply. In February 1972 steps were also taken to reduce those interest rates that were officially fixed. At these new levels they were scarcely above the rate of inflation that was being experienced and expected, so that (especially after tax) lenders holding government bonds or fixed-interest deposits with banks were effectively obtaining a very low or even negative real return. The stimulus that this low cost of borrowing provided for businesses to undertake new investment was thus accompanied by a strong stimulus to lenders to move out of such financial assets into real estate (and other durable goods). If the stimulus to activity had been given instead mainly by tax cuts or subsidies (and less by an expansion of the money supply, with consequent reductions in interest rates) this stimulus to land prices and this discouragement to the holding of financial assets would not have been so great.

Through a mixture of bad luck in matters outside its control—especially world stagflation and the unexpected rise in the propensity to save in Australia—and bad judgment, the macro-economic policy performance of the Liberal-Country Party government in 1971–2 rated very poorly. Unemployment had risen much higher than was intended and inflation was far more serious than at any time since 1951. The exchange rate had been allowed to become seriously undervalued and the resulting capital inflow contributed to bringing about a dangerously rapid rise in the money supply, to which monetary policy in late 1971 also contributed. The right policy mix would have been an upward revaluation of the dollar (or substantial tariff cuts) accompanied by large-scale tax cuts, possibly with some rise in government spending. Some increase in the rate of expansion of the money supply, sufficient to accommodate the rising real level of activity would presumably have been required, but the far more rapid rise in the money supply that was in fact permitted merely ensured that a real estate boom and an incipient flight from financial assets would follow. In short, what was wanted was lower tax rates, higher interest rates (rather than lower ones) and an appreciation (or tariff cuts).

This prescription was followed, belatedly, only in part by the budget of August 1972. This provided for substantial tax cuts and some considerable increases in government spending, these being mainly indirectly by way of encouragement for state government expenditure rather than by way of Commonwealth outlays on goods and services. If this had been accompanied immediately by a substantial appreciation, the expansionary effect, coupled with the reduction of cost-push inflation that could be expected to result from the tax cuts, might well have alleviated the problem of cost-push inflation coupled with unemployment. As it was, the further postponement of the revaluation meant that the monetary effects of the budgetary expansion were excessive, as they were accompanied by a further expansion of the money supply as more capital poured in, despite certain measures to restrain particular types of inflow (a prohibition in September 1972 of fixed-interest borrowing overseas for periods of less than two years), which had the effect of diverting the inflow into new forms and new channels, at the cost of increasing the real cost to the country of a given level of capital inflow.

Furthermore, during the second half of 1972 the economy began to recover. Indeed, the recovery started about the time that the budget was introduced to provide a substantial additional expansionary force. A rapid rise in disposable incomes, as well as a recovery in the proportion of them devoted to consumption, played an important part in the recovery in demand, but a rapid increase in farm incomes, resulting partly from strong world markets for farm products, also contributed. But expenditure on private fixed capital equipment continued to be sluggish, though dwelling construction was booming.

Meanwhile, the rate of inflation continued to be high, partly because of the undervalued exchange rate, for this meant that Australia had failed to use the main instrument available for insulating herself against the quickening inflation in the outside world. The strength of the Australian balance of payments in 1971 had presumably been one major influence upon the decision of the Arbitration Commission to award an unusually large rise in wage rates at that time, so that the mechanism used to adjust to the strong balance of payments was the inflationary one of rises in money incomes in Australia instead of the anti-inflationary one of an appreciation.

Labor Government: Recovery, Boom and Hyper-stagflation

The return of a Labor government in December 1972—the first for twenty-three years—brought initially a number of quick and firm decisions. One of the first of these, in December 1972, was the revaluation of the Australian dollar to a more appropriate level. But it is worth emphasizing that, whatever the political complexion of the government returned to power at that time, some such move would have been unavoidable. At the same time, with much less justification (if any), the government introduced a Variable Deposit Requirement (originally at 25 per cent) on fixed-interest borrowing from overseas, which effectively increased substantially the cost of any such borrowing, as the borrower had to make an interest-free deposit with the Reserve Bank equal to the stated percentage of the sum borrowed overseas. Presumably this measure was introduced in order to discourage a further speculative inflow if people were not convinced that no further revaluation was likely. But even if one accepted that some such measure could serve a useful short-term purpose, it was bound (like the prohibition on short-term overseas borrowing for less than two years, which had been introduced by the previous government) mainly to have the effect of diverting capital inflow into less preferred, and therefore presumably more costly, channels.

In any event, at the effective exchange rate established by February 1973 it could not reasonably be argued that people might take the view that the Australian exchange rate was undervalued. For in that month the U.S. dollar was devalued and the Australian dollar (quite rightly) was not devalued with it. This amounted to a further small appreciation of the Australian dollar in terms of the average of major currencies. That would have been a good moment to abandon the fixed link with the (now effectively floating) U.S. dollar, and scrap the Variable Deposit Requirement; but in fact it was continued (at various rates) until the second half of 1974, despite the fact that by then the situation had changed to an expectation that the Australian dollar might be devalued. For over the two years 1973–4 the external picture changed from excessive surplus to considerable deficit. If an expectation of an upward revaluation was accepted as grounds for imposing the deposit requirement late in 1972, the prevalence of the view in 1974 that a devaluation was likely and that this might result in capital outflow would logically have constituted grounds not merely for the removal of the deposit requirement but even for paying a subsidy on overseas borrowing in 1974. But in fact such official interferences in either direction with particular types of capital flows on macro-economic grounds are to be deplored as both costly and ineffective—at least in anything but the very short run—and no substitute for a rational exchange rate policy.

Internally the recovery of 1972–3, which led to full (or even overfull) employment, gave way by the end of 1974 with quite remarkable suddenness to the highest level of unemployment, yet also the most rapid inflation, since World War II. These changes in the internal situation broadly paralleled those in the world economy generally, but Australia had much less excuse for allowing her economy to become so subject to them than had other developed countries. Just as the record of the Liberal-Country Party government was wide open to criticism in 1971–2, it could equally well be argued that by the end of 1974 the sum of the measures adopted by the new government almost added up to a model of how not to operate macro-economic policy in world where high rates of unemployment and high rates of inflation were occurring simultaneously.

Initially the Labor government that came to power late in 1972 took the right decisions on the major matter of the exchange rate; but it failed to take steps to ensure that the rate then remained appropriate, which could best have been done by allowing the rate to become more flexible (as most major countries were doing), either by introducing a foreign exchange market or by frequent changes of the official rate (in combination with other instruments of policy), in such a way as to prevent the reserves from rising unduly high or falling unduly low. This it failed to do in the first half of 1973, when the result of keeping the rate for the Australian dollar fixed in terms of the U.S. dollar was that, as the latter happened to depreciate over the period February to July 1973 in terms of other currencies, the Australian dollar also depreciated in a period when Australia's reserves were still high and her balance of payments strong (despite the official limitations on capital inflow). It is true that the government improved the situation by tariff cuts in July, and then by a further appreciation in September. But in the meantime it had by its actions—especially in the matter of public service salaries and its evidence in the national wage case—given a further stimulus to wage-cost inflation in Australia, which the inappropriately valued exchange rate in the first half of 1973 also exacerbated by raising the price level in Australia. At the same time, the various expansionary forces at work in the economy at the time the Labor government came to power had brought the economy up to, or close to, full employment, so that demand inflation was now being added to cost-push inflation. It is true that unemployment rates were not as low as in former periods of boom, but most other indicators were such as to imply full employment. The interpretation of cyclical indicators presented difficulties at the time, but the economy certainly reached by mid-1973 a situation where the main problem seemed to be the prevention of excess demand.

One very buoyant sector was that of building, which had been stimulated by the ready availability of finance and by the strong pressure to move out of money and other financial assets into real assets such as buildings at a time when real interest rates were negative. If the lessons of earlier booms had been taken to heart, this situation would not have been allowed to arise. In 1973 the rate of inflation was much higher than it had been in earlier booms, and the level of nominal interest rates needed to yield a positive real post-tax return to the lender was therefore much higher. Yet politicians and journalists persisted in speaking of interest rates as 'high', meaning, of course, that *nominal* interest rates were high. The failure to adjust rates upwards fast enough to offset people's expectations of a higher rate of inflation made the inflation worse, as it further stimulated the move out of money assets into real assets and reduced the availability of funds to businesses. It also meant (just as it had in earlier booms) that still greater rises in nominal interest rates would have to occur eventually as inflation consequently became worse.

The main political obstacle to an adequate upward adjustment in nominal interest rates was the political strength of those purchasing their homes on mortgages. But if it was felt necessary to protect such individuals in the immediate future from the full force of higher interest rates (despite the fact that they were one of the groups likely to benefit most in the long run from borrowing at negative real interest rates), the appropriate way to do this would have been temporary loans to see them through this period or some form of subsidization of their repayments of principal or interest. It was quite indefensible to hold the general level of interest rates and the post-tax return to lenders at levels that were absurdly low (considered in the light of double-digit inflation) merely in order to protect a particular group of borrowers. Such a policy was closely parallel to the maintenance of an undervalued exchange rate in 1972 as a concealed subsidy to Country Party supporters. A straight-out subsidy to the sectional interests concerned would have been far more efficient for the purpose and less damaging to the country's economy than keeping a major instrument of macro-economic policy at a level at which lower living standards and more inflation than was necessary were consequently inflicted on the whole country.

Nevertheless, increases in a range of nominal interest rates were made in September and October 1973, and a severe curtailment of credit, including that for housing, was made—far too late and far too drastically as it turned out. (Again, the lessons of earlier periods when interest rates were not raised until far too late had not been properly learned.)

In one sense the credit squeeze of 1973–4 was far too drastic, if one means by this that it contributed towards bringing about the most severe post-war recession. That is to say, given the setting of the other macro-economic instruments it would have been better if the credit squeeze had been less severe. But there is no reason why the setting of the other instruments should be assumed unalterable. What was required was a drastic cut in tax rates, coupled with a *raising* of interest rates to a level that would yield lenders a positive real post-tax return. Given also a sufficiently expansionary budgetary policy to restore and maintain full employment by tax reduction aimed at reducing cost-inflation, this would have made lenders much readier to supply funds to industry, and industry much readier to borrow them and use them to finance higher outlays. By contrast, the policy followed severely held down the availability of credit for business, even though the nominal interest rates that had to be paid when credit could be obtained were not really high in the context of a rate of inflation of the order of 20 per cent per annum. But the high rates of taxation paid both by lenders and by companies— including taxation levied on profits that were fictional rather than real—made it hard for companies to pay even these low or negative real interest rates, when lenders were willing to offer them funds.[1] It is not surprising that in such conditions the capital market ceased to operate properly and that recession and serious inflation occurred together.

The swift transition from high activity in 1973 to recession (with the highest level of unemployment in Australia since the 1930s) in 1974 was due to a combination of factors.(Indeed, the sharpness of the decline in the rate of growth of activity in 1974 was in marked contrast to the smoother fluctuations of earlier years.) At the global level it was part of the reduction in the level

---

[1] Profits as calculated for tax purposes exceeded real profits in periods of inflation, because the rise in the prices of stocks of goods and equipment held by companies could not be deducted from their apparent profits in calculating their tax liability.

of activity in most countries, partly resulting from governments everywhere continuing to apply measures appropriate to checking excess demand as a remedy for types of inflation that now had their main cause on the cost side. Among these cost influences was the very high price now charged for oil by oil exporters, from the effects of which Australia was largely shielded as a result of the high proportion of her oil requirements now met from her own output. But the continued rise in money incomes in most countries stemmed largely from the period of high activity virtually everywhere in 1973 and from the rapid rise in food prices that this generated, after remarkably widespread harvest failures. This rise in food prices was, or should have been, helpful to Australia, as a food exporter, in *avoiding* inflation, if the consequent improvement in her terms of trade had been allowed to lead to a correspondingly higher volume of imports.

The ready availability of supplies from other countries contributed to the very high volume of imports into Australia much later, however, in 1974, when it presented serious problems for import-competing industries and helped to raise the level of unemployment, as tax rates were not reduced fast enough to absorb the imports and still maintain something closer to full employment. At the same time, dwelling construction was adversely affected by the credit stringency introduced in 1973, as was also the level of business activity. Furthermore, the high rate of inflation had the effect of greatly increasing tax receipts, presumably above the level that the government had expected. This was only partly because the method of accounting used by companies (and applied in taxing them) tends to overstate the real level of profits during inflation (through allowing insufficient provision for the higher cost of replacing stocks and fixed assets).[2] It was also because the very high rate of inflation pushed individuals sharply upwards on the tax scale and so made income-tax receipts rise much faster than incomes generally. Some official advisers apparently advocated a short, sharp rise in unemployment as a means of checking inflation. Although the government apparently did not accept this view, it raised post office charges and some excise duties, and unemployment in fact rose by late 1974 to the sort of level that the advocates of this view had proposed.

The attempt to hold down the rate of inflation by making major companies refer proposed price increases to the Prices Justification Tribunal (established in 1973) also made it difficult for companies to maintain the post-tax level of their profits. This made them reluctant to undertake new investment programmes; and the outlook for post-tax returns for lenders, especially in real terms, was so poor that it would have been hard for companies to raise fixed-interest capital even if they had been prepared to do so. With high and unpredictable rates of inflation and high marginal tax rates, the capital markets of the world were ceasing to function efficiently. No one knows what is a reasonable rate of interest to offer or demand when no one can say, within a very wide margin, what the rate of inflation will be. This constitutes part of the case for introducing financial assets with repayments (whether interest, principal or both) linked to some index of inflation. This might be best introduced by governments offering a bond with some form of index-linking. Certainly if political conditions make it hard to raise those interest rates under official

---

[2] The situation was alleviated only very slightly by certain temporary measures late in 1974.

control to a nominal level appropriate to people's expectations about the rate of inflation, index-linking would be a way of establishing an appropriate real interest rate that might be more acceptable. Private firms might follow this example if governments took the lead in this matter. It would also have the advantage of reducing the nominal rates of interest automatically once the rate of inflation started to fall, whereas if long-term interest rates were raised to levels at which they fully reflected people's inflationary expectations, it might be much harder to prevent a dangerous rise in real interest rates occurring once the rate of inflation was checked.

Internal considerations thus reinforce the external case that could be made in the mid-1970s for the Australian government to offer a positive real rate of return to attract some of the vast sums of oil money ('petro-dollars') seeking a profitable outlet. For it would be difficult (as well as undesirable) to offer index-linked loans to overseas investors without also offering them to lenders within Australia. The availability of financial assets with a positive return even in conditions of inflation is one necessary pre-condition for making capital markets function properly again, as well as for stemming or forestalling a flight from money and from assets denominated in money terms, which is the main characteristic of hyper-inflation. With rates of inflation around 20 per cent in Australia and elsewhere at the end of 1974, this was clearly the form of inflation most to be feared. Major financial innovations seemed likely to be needed if hyper-inflation were to be avoided, and the policies framed solely or mainly with an eye to meeting the last form of inflation but one (excess demand) or even the more recent form (cost-inflation) were unlikely to be adequate to cope with it. But remarkably little public attention seemed to have been given to this crucial matter in Australia. Perhaps it was inhibited by a fear that discussion of it might make hyper-inflation worse, by further encouraging the flight from money and financial assets.

In summary, the basic aim should be to return to a situation where holders of financial assets can count on normally being able to obtain a positive real post-tax return on their savings. This involves some combination of reducing the rate of tax on these returns and allowing interest rates and post-tax company earnings to rise —whilst of course ensuring by adequate tax cuts and subsidies that the level of activity does not fall below what is felt to be desirable. Index-linked obligations should probably play a part in such a programme, and if Australia adopted such measures she would almost certainly attract a level of capital inflow that would make possible a substantial appreciation or cut in tariffs (which should again be appropriately offset as to their internal effects by expansionary budgetary and monetary measures).

One factor that made it especially hard to avoid inflation in Australia was the much less receptive attitude of the new government towards capital inflow, and the continuance (until the second half of 1974) of both the prohibition on short-term overseas borrowing for less than two years (reduced to six months late in 1974) and the Variable Deposit Requirement (increased to 33½ per cent during 1973, reduced to 25 per cent early in 1974 and then to the nominal level of 5 per cent in August, and finally reduced to zero in November 1974). These measures diverted the flow of capital into less preferred (and therefore presumably more costly) channels, and may well have held down the level of capital inflow; whilst the change in official attitudes certainly did so. Confused thinking about the allegedly inflationary effects of capital inflow was apparently behind this. Yet capital inflow makes possible the purchase of a higher level of imports than could otherwise have been afforded and is not inflationary if used for this, its proper, purpose. Only so far as the government fails to adopt the appropriate setting of its macro-economic instruments (including the exchange rate) to see that this occurs will capital inflow be inflationary. Of course, much of the capital inflow that occurred in 1972 appeared to be inflationary, in the sense that it could not all be used to make possible a higher level of imports, as much of it was bound to be reversed when the exchange rate was revalued upwards to a more appropriate level. But in this case also it was therefore the inappropriate exchange rate, rather than the capital inflow, that caused the inflation. In 1973–4 it was the government's measures to prevent capital inflow of types that might have come in (and which could then have been used to permit a higher level of imports) that was inflationary. Had these measures limiting capital inflow been scrapped—as they should have been—early in 1973 and any consequent extra capital inflow been used to pay for a higher level of imports, by way of more appreciation (or bigger tariff cuts) than actually occurred, the rate of inflation in 1973–4 could have been less. The extent of the muddled thinking on this matter was also exemplified by the presentation of the relaxation and eventual removal of the Variable Deposit Requirement in 1974 as being a means of increasing the liquidity of the economy. For it should certainly not have been used for this purpose, which can be fulfilled by tax cuts, subsidies or easier credit. Extra capital inflow is justifiable only to make possible a higher level of imports—by bringing about more appreciation (or less depreciation) or more tariff cuts than would otherwise have occurred. It should not, therefore, be allowed to add to domestic liquidity, even though individual firms may of course find that it helps their liquidity to have access to it.

There may also have been a further form of muddled thinking about the capital inflow controls. There appears to have been confusion in some politicians' minds of the effects of these restrictions with the very different matter of limiting overseas control of industries in Australia. But the controls over fixed-interest borrowing hurt mainly Australian-owned and controlled firms, which had much less scope to borrow from overseas in other ways than did the Australian branches and subsidiaries of multi-national companies. (This point was eventually acknowledged officially in the middle of 1974 in the announcement of the relaxation of the Variable Deposit Requirement.)

The devaluation of September 1974 was almost as misguided as the Liberal-Country Party government's exchange rate policy in 1972. It is true that imports had risen very rapidly in 1973–4 and the reserves had fallen sharply—though from an unduly high level. Certainly, if they had gone on falling at that rate something would have eventually had to be done. But there was much evidence that a good deal of the rise in imports was temporary and that the credit stringency within Australia would shortly reduce them. Moreover, capital inflow was still being forcibly held down by the continuance until the second half of 1974 of the Variable Deposit Requirement and by the prohibition on borrowing for less than two years. (These were imposed to check capital *inflow* at a time when *appreciation* was expected.) The former was abolished only belatedly and the latter was changed late in 1974 to a prohibition on borrowing for less than six months, but by then it had become more difficult to attract capital inflow. Moreover, the level of the reserves and balance of payments situation had by then made it difficult to attract the sort of level of capital inflow that might have been both feasible and desirable from Australia's point of view, especially from oil-exporting countries which were looking for suitable outlets for their accumulating foreign exchange. A more appropriate remedy would have been for Australia to search actively for such capital, offering it positive real rates of return by the issue of bonds with a return linked to some index of inflation.

It was in any case probable that devaluation had by now become much less useful as a balance of payments weapon, for in the current inflationary climate it was liable before long to lead to a further stimulus to domestic inflation, perhaps on almost the same scale as the devaluation itself, so that the real state of the current account would not in the medium run be favourably affected to any great extent.

Moreover, the devaluation of September 1974 was undertaken at least partly for its internal effects, and for these purposes also it was in the short run likely to be worse than useless. For so far as it succeeded in stimulating domestic activity, this would occur only when, with a lag of some months, the volume of imports started to fall and perhaps that of some exports began to rise in response to the devaluation. Furthermore, this would be a beggar-my-neighbour remedy for unemployment such as was roundly condemned in the 1930s, at a time when the world economy was once again threatened by a serious recession which was likely to intensify if countries exported their unemployment to each other. Moreover, in the new situation where high rates of inflation accompanied the unemployment the most confident prediction one could make about the effects of a devaluation was that it would make the price level rise faster in the country applying it—and that this would occur at once, well before the volume of trade started to respond to the devaluation.

So far as the aim was to improve the level of domestic activity rather than to reduce the external deficit, it could be argued that devaluation was not even a very efficient way of beggaring Australia's neighbours. A far more appropriate way of doing so would have been to subsidize those few industries that were adversely affected by imports, or even assist them by import controls. For subsidies would tend to hold down the rate of increase in the price level within Australia, thus contributing towards the major aim of reducing the rate of inflation. Instead of subsidizing those industries that were felt to be politically sensitive (so far as it felt obliged to do so), however, the government introduced not only the devaluation but also subsequently certain tariff measures and measures of import control which inevitably had the effect of further increasing the rate of inflation within Australia.

So far as there was a valid case for devaluation on balance of payments grounds, it is true that to that extent it would not have been a beggar-my-neighbour remedy for unemployment. But the devaluation seemed far greater than could be justified by external considerations—especially in view of the continued restrictions on capital inflow. If the political necessity had to be accepted to avoid further reductions in employment in textiles and other industries adversely affected by imports, the appropriate remedy would have been subsidies for these industries, rather than devaluation, tariffs or import controls, though if taxes had been kept low enough to avoid general unemployment this would not have been a problem. Indeed, a major aim of the government should have been to eliminate tariffs as quickly as possible and substitute subsidies so far as it took the view that the existing pattern of industry had to be preserved. This would have helped to reduce the rate of inflation. But the basic difficulty was that the government had failed to adopt sufficiently sweeping measures to retrain and resettle manpower released by the tariff cuts of 1973, or to maintain a sufficiently high level of activity to ensure that they were absorbed elsewhere.

The world events that led to a rise in unemployment and in rates of inflation in most countries during 1973–4 need not have been allowed to bring about the same combination of problems in Australia if interest rates had been allowed to rise, if capital had been admitted freely, if the dollar had been revalued upwards further and sooner (or tariffs cut appropriately), and tax rates reduced (instead of effectively increased). For Australia, virtually alone among developed countries, was well placed to benefit from both the high food prices in 1973 and the high fuel prices in 1973–4, and also to attract capital from the countries flush with petro-dollars. Other countries had far more serious macro-economic problems for reasons beyond their own control. Australia's distinctive contribution to macro-economic policy during the period was to have got herself into an appalling macro-economic mess when there was no fundamental economic reason why this should have occurred. The main reason why this happened was a lack of clear thinking on the exchange rate, interest rates, tax rates and the relationship between capital inflow and inflation.

Prices and incomes policy

In contrast to most comparable countries, Australia did not for many years attempt to apply anything that could really be called a prices and incomes policy. This was partly because of constitutional difficulties and partly because of scepticism as to the efficacy of attempts by governments to control the rate of increase of the price level or money incomes generally. The Arbitration Commission judgments may have had some partial effect in this direction in the 1950s and 1960s, and so far as the statements made to the commission by the Commonwealth government may have influenced its decisions some might argue that Australia had for many years had some such policy. But in fact the Arbitration Commission judgments applied only to certain wage incomes and not to incomes generally, and they were in any event about various minimum rates, whereas the essence of a prices and incomes policy as normally understood is that it is concerned with maximum incomes: that is, with restraining the rate of increase in money incomes. In a sense, therefore, one could regard Australia's reliance on the Arbitration Commission as the very antithesis of an incomes policy, especially when in the early 1970s it seemed increasingly to lose control of the level of actual earnings, and in many cases it was merely sanctioning 'consent' awards already reached by the parties.

But the Labor government made certain moves during 1973 and 1974 that might be thought of as coming into the category of a prices and incomes policy. There was first its setting up of the Prices Justification Tribunal in 1973, which had the power to consider and make recommendations upon proposed price increases by major firms. It did not have the power to forbid proposed price increases (though it could impose penalties for infringements), but in fact its decisions were adhered to by all the firms concerned. Whatever effect this had on particular prices, however, it is by no means certain that this did much, if anything, to hold down the rate of increase in the general price level. It certainly made it harder for the firms whose prices were held down to secure a post-tax return at which it was profitable to maintain their level of operations. It therefore undoubtedly contributed towards the sharp reduction in business confidence and investment during 1974.

The referendum at the end of 1973 at which the government was denied the power to control prices and incomes would have removed the constitutional barriers to operating a prices and incomes policy. But if the referendum had been successful, the vital issue would have been whether such a policy would have been applied to incomes (the granting of which power was opposed by the unions) or only to prices. If the latter had been done, the probability would have been that this would still further have depressed business activity. On the other hand, a successful policy to control all incomes would have brought down prices indirectly—though the political obstacles to implementing such a policy would presumably have ruled it out, even if one could assume that it would otherwise have been feasible.

The government announced in 1974 its intention to recommend to the Arbitration Commission the re-introduction of adjustments of award wage rates according to the cost of living. This measure may or may not check the rate of increase in money wage rates and therefore prices, according to whether wage settlements would otherwise have been higher than those reached under such a system. The argument in favour of such a system is the hope that after its introduction unions will moderate their wage demands, as they will not then have to build into their demands an allowance for an unknown rate of increase in the price level. But there is no certainty—some would say no reasonable probability—that money wage demands will be held back to the full extent of the extra payments resulting from such indexing of money wage rates. If wage settlements other than that part of wages linked to the price index are not moderated to a fully offsetting extent, any such arrangements will make wage inflation worse. One possible solution may be to pay the index-linked wage increase only to people whose money incomes have since the last index-linked award risen by less than the index (or perhaps by some stated flat percentage in excess of the adjustment).

The experience of other countries suggests that the successful application of prices and incomes policies is difficult, at least in anything but the short run. If all other macro-economic instruments are also being rationally applied to minimizing the rate of increase of prices and money incomes (at a given level of activity), a prices and incomes policy may well play a useful supplementary role. But if that is being done, prices and incomes policies may well not be needed. In short, the amount of attention that has been devoted to the hypothetical question of how to operate such policies in Australia might better be diverted to securing a proper use and appropriate combinations of the macro-economic instruments that are already available—especially the rate of interest, tax rates and the exchange rate. For unless rational policies are adopted on those matters, prices and incomes policies will certainly fail. There is also a risk that if a government is trying to apply a prices and incomes policy for which it hopes or expects success, it will be more likely to continue to keep its interest rates, tax rates or exchange rates at levels that cannot reasonably be expected to minimize the rate of inflation. But once it faces up to the political problems involved in using these weapons properly, it might be reasonable to introduce some sort of temporary prices and incomes restraint to speed up the process of returning to price stability.

TABLE 1

Quarterly indicators of movements in the Australian economy, 1962-74

| | | Registered unemployed* ('000) | Registered vacancies* ('000) | Percentage change in twelve months to the stated quarter | | |
				Gross National Expenditure	Money supply	Consumer price index
1962	March	101	20	-2.7	6.9	-0.1
	June	94	23	-8.5	7.5	-0.8
	September	94	24	12.4	7.9	-0.1
	December	92	25	13.7	7.9	0.1
1963	March	85	27	9.5	7.9	0.3
	June	83	27	8.5	8.6	0.7
	September	77	29	7.8	9.0	0.6
	December	67	34	7.6	10.5	0.5
1964	March	60	38	6.9	11.7	1.0
	June	52	45	10.5	12.1	1.7
	September	47	50	13.5	12.9	2.7
	December	45	50	12.7	11.6	4.0
1965	March	43	54	17.9	9.9	4.0
	June	42	57	14.2	8.2	4.1
	September	43	54	9.2	5.9	3.9
	December	51	51	6.6	5.2	4.0
1966	March	57	46	2.0	4.9	3.4
	June	59	43	2.9	5.8	3.3
	September	63	42	2.8	7.3	2.7
	December	64	43	7.2	7.7	2.4
1967	March	64	41	12.5	8.1	2.8
	June	67	39	9.3	8.1	2.8
	September	69	36	8.2	8.4	3.9
	December	66	35	7.9	9.0	3.3
1968	March	68	37	5.9	7.8	3.1
	June	68	37	10.8	8.3	3.1
	September	65	38	11.2	7.7	1.9
	December	64	37	12.6	7.0	2.6
1969	March	62	39	10.6	8.6	2.9
	June	58	43	10.0	9.1	2.9
	September	54	47	9.4	8.9	3.1
	December	57	49	6.8	9.5	2.8
1970	March	52	54	8.6	8.4	3.2
	June	50	54	11.7	6.2	3.7
	September	58	48	9.3	5.4	3.8
	December	43	48	8.9	5.1	4.9
1971	March	64	46	13.5	5.5	4.9
	June	67	41	10.3	6.1	5.4
	September	77	39	11.0	7.9	6.7
	December	87	37	11.4	8.3	7.2
1972	March	96	32	6.6	10.2	7.1
	June	102	31	9.6	10.2	6.2
	September	114	32	6.8	13.3	5.7
	December	107	34	8.8	18.3	4.5
1973	March	90	48	9.4	21.8	5.7
	June	89	62	14.8	24.7	8.2
	September	85	76	21.0	25.3	10.6
	December	84	72	24.8	21.9	13.2
1974	March	85	82	30.7	19.3	13.6
	June	82	85	24.1	16.2	14.4
	September	123	50	20.9	8.1	16.0
	December	214	36	21.7	9.6	16.3

*Seasonally adjusted.
SOURCE: Commonwealth Bureau of Census and Statistics and *Australian Economic Review*

FIGURE 1

Quarterly Indicators, 1962–74

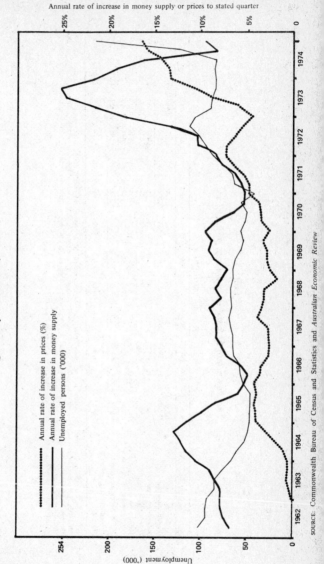

SOURCE: Commonwealth Bureau of Census and Statistics and *Australian Economic Review*

TABLE 2

The Australian balance of payments, 1961/62 to 1973/74

($ million)

	1961/2	1962/3	1963/4	1964/5	1965/6	1966/7	1967/8	1968/9	1969/70	1970/1	1971/2	1972/3	1973/4
Visible exports	2,128	2,121	2,730	2,574	2,626	2,926	2,941	3,217	3,981	4,217	4,726	5,991	6,719
Visible imports	1,701	2,065	2,237	2,739	2,822	2,837	3,159	3,203	3,584	3,790	3,792	3,808	5,750
Balance of trade	+427	+56	+493	−165	−196	+89	−218	+14	+397	+427	+934	+2,183	+969
Net invisibles	−429	−519	−541	−511	−688	−740	−905	−1,020	−1,277	−1,276	−1,309	−1,483	−1,706
Balance on current account	−2	−463	−48	−776	−884	−651	−1,123	−1,006	−830	−849	−375	699	−737
Net apparent capital inflow	180	614	498	480	941	527	1,202	1,154	867	1,447	1,818	379	168
Net monetary movements	+178	+151	+450	−296	+57	−124	+79	+148	+37	+598	+1,422	+1,079	−569
Official reserve assets at end of year	1,162	1,313	1,763	1,467	1,447	1,315	1,277	1,514	1,638	2,329	3,734	4,254	3,417

NOTE: The changes in the figures for official reserve assets differ from the line marked 'Net monetary movements' in the table, as the former reflects also the fall in the value of reserves resulting from devaluations in 1967, as well as changes in the I.M.F. gold tranche and the issue of Special Drawing Rights in 1970. The net balance on monetary movements shown in the balance of payments reflects changes in reserve assets owned by the banking system as well as those in official reserve assets.

SOURCE: Commonwealth Bureau of Census and Statistics, Balance of Payments.

FIGURE 2

External Accounts, 1962–74

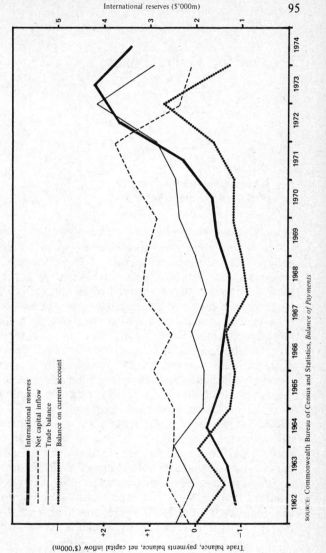

International reserves ($'000m)

Trade balance, payments balance, net capital inflow ($'000m)

International reserves
Net capital inflow
Trade balance
Balance on current account

SOURCE: Commonwealth Bureau of Census and Statistics, *Balance of Payments*

Lessons for Future Policy

I. Lessons from the experience of the 1950s and 1960s

Budgetary compared with monetary measures

In drawing upon past experience as a guide to future policy, the relative advantages and deficiences of budgetary and monetary measures have to be borne in mind. Although the predictability of the effects of budgetary measures has perhaps at times been exaggerated, it remains true that they can be tailored more exactly than can monetary measures to achieve a given total effect and a given distribution of it between different industries and income groups. Efforts should therefore constantly be made to continue and extend the degree of flexibility of budgetary measures that was achieved in Australia over the course of the 1950s and 1960s. In particular, the readiness to vary income tax cyclically and even more than once in the course of a year should be carried further, so that such variations come to be accepted as a normal measure and not merely one for use in extreme circumstances. But it has to be assumed that measures of tax policy will continue to be less than ideally flexible, however much progress there may be in that direction. Some progress seems also to have been made in speeding up and slowing down government expenditure with changing conditions during the 1960s. But it has been suggested that blueprints for extra public works were not readily available to be brought into action quickly on the scale that would have been desirable during the 1961 recession; the range of blueprints available in the 1952–3 recession seems to have been on a scale facilitating quicker action on this front.

The fluctuations of demand to which the Australian economy is subject make it especially difficult to judge at all exactly what degree of government restraint or stimulation will be required over any period of twelve months. An August budget must in part aim at the average effect its framers expect to be required over the next twelve months; but it should pay special attention to the first six months or so of the period, and if the greater risk in that six-month period is of overfull employment it should run the risk of erring, if at all, in an anti-inflationary direction. There can be no objection to this approach provided that there is the intention of varying the budgetary or monetary measures within six months or so to meet any change in the situation; and this means that budgetary measures may have to be varied within a year, unless it is felt that monetary measures alone can meet the changes that occur before the next annual budget. It would be a pity if uninformed criticism of frequent variations of policy (sometimes described disparagingly as 'stop-go') were to prevent the adoption of suitably flexible policies. For the more frequent the variations of policy, the more effective will budgetary and monetary measures usually be in keeping the economy fairly near to the knife edge of full employment without inflation.

It will probably remain true that monetary measures

can be more frequently varied than budgetary measures, though the speed and efficacy of monetary measures in achieving their effects will remain open to doubt. The important thing is that the central bank and the government should together take any early action that is deemed desirable. In the period under review there were occasions (at least during the 1950s) when one suspected that the central bank and the government (or the Treasury) were not always at one; but it must be added that the Canberra and Sydney arms of the monetary authorities seemed to be working in closer harmony during the 1960s.

The other major point to be made about monetary weapons is that doubts and disagreement about the extent of their efficacy in various circumstances need not and should not inhibit their use. If they are weak in their effects, this is at least as good an argument for using them in a forthright manner as for placing greater reliance on budgetary measures. In fact, of course, the important things is that budgetary and monetary measures should be used to reinforce each other as far as possible; but that where a deliberate choice is made to place prime reliance on one group of measures—for instance, the budgetary ones—the logic of the position must be accepted; namely, that this means that the budgetary measures that are to be stressed must indeed be used in a very much more forthright manner (and a much more flexible and timely way) than would have been necessary if equal stress had been placed on both budgetary and monetary measures. But in practice political and administrative difficulties often delay the taking of budgetary action. When this is so, principal reliance may have to be placed upon monetary measures for early and minor corrections, and especially for adjustment between annual, or possibly twice-yearly changes in budgetary policy.

The greater the flexibility of budgetary measures that proves politically and administratively feasible, therefore, the less the weight that will need to be placed on the more readily variable, but generally less reliable, monetary measures. But if budgetary measures are in this sense to be regarded as the senior partner, one must not proceed from this view to suggest that a flexible use of monetary measures can therefore be avoided. The overriding maxim must be that *though monetary measures can never be depended upon to achieve any major correction by themselves, it is vital that they should never be pulling in the wrong direction.* In particular, those interest rates under official control or influence must never be permitted to lag seriously behind cyclical movements in the general level of uncontrolled interest rates. (There is, however, room for flexibility and choice in deciding how far variations in controlled rates should be used to lead variations in the general level of interest rates, and how far variations in budgetary policy should be preferred. Again, the greater the degree of budgetary flexibility that proves feasible, the less will be the need to employ variations in controlled interest rates to lead the market.)

By the middle 1960s many of the principal obstacles in the way of choosing an appropriate combination of budgetary and monetary measures had diminished in importance to a point where they were, on balance, probably no greater (and perhaps even less) than in any country in the Anglo-Saxon world, and indeed, beyond it. In particular, the widespread acceptance and understanding by the major parties and by informed opinion of the principles of 'Keynesian' budgeting cleared away one obstacle that has continued to limit budgetary policy in the United States and in several continental European countries.[1] It is true that relics of pre-Keynesian thinking were still to be found in newspaper comment in Australia in 1964: a good example was the suggestion made in some papers that the high level of tax receipts (resulting from a high level of activity and, indeed, the danger of excess demand) justified a reduction in tax rates in the 1964 budget. In fact, of course, the rise in private spending that caused much of the rise in tax receipts provided a strong argument for raising tax rates in order to prevent excess demand. But though such unsophisticated comments may continue at times to colour the views of some journalists and politicians, such attitudes no longer seemed, from the mid-1960s onwards, to be a serious obstacle to the taking of appropriate budgetary action in Australia—though they may well have been so in the past, even up to the late 1950s.

Choice of monetary measures

Similarly, many of the obstacles to the use of monetary measures that hampered policy well into the 1960s seemed to have diminished by about the mid-1960s. Indeed, the scope for applying appropriate measures of monetary policy in Australia seemed, on balance, by then to be at least as great as in any other country (even if due allowance is made for certain constitutional limitations in Australia upon the powers of the federal government and central bank).

For, in the first place, the central bank in Australia

[1] The American tax cuts eventually applied in 1964 had seemed to indicate that this sort of obstacle had become less serious in the United States. But on several occasions in subsequent years changes in budgetary policy directed at macro-economic objectives were delayed unduly because of the difficulty of persuading Congress of the need for them.

had in effect from 1960 onwards unlimited powers to control bank liquidity directly through S.R.D.s (though political difficulties might somewhat limit their use in practice)—provided that it gave the statutory notice. By contrast, the use of this weapon in Britain (whose Special Deposits system had been used very little) was limited by traditional attitudes and some institutional difficulties, and in the United States by statutory limitations. In a sense the wide powers of the Australian central bank to control bank liquidity directly were to some extent an obstacle to securing the appropriate blend of monetary measures, in that in the past undue reliance had at times been placed upon this weapon, though the danger of this seemed to be diminishing with the revival of interest-rate policy, open-market operations, and budgetary measures from 1964 onwards. In addition, the effective powers of control of the Australian central bank exceeded those of its counterparts in Britain and North America by reason of the conventional agreement with the trading banks about a minimum L.G.S. ratio. For so long as this agreement can be depended upon (or perhaps even made statutory, if necessary), this must help to restrict or eliminate any 'shift' on the part of the trading banks out of bonds into advances in times of a 'credit squeeze'—a problem that has at times hampered central banks elsewhere.[2]

Against these greater powers enjoyed by the Australian central bank, one must set the consideration that the central bank in Australia was more restricted than its counterparts in Britain and America—at least up to about the mid-1960s—by the more limited bond

---

[2] The Bank of England attempted on occasions to overcome this problem by telling the banks that it expected them to react to measures reducing their liquidity mainly by reducing their advances rather than their bond holdings.

market, and by the limited (though growing) scale of the official short-term money market (established only in 1959). But by 1964 the range of short-term and long-term government obligations outstanding in Australia, and the greater scope for dealing in them (partly a result of the growth of the official short-term money market to the point where portfolio limits were removed in 1964) meant that this handicap had been steadily diminishing. Moreover, in a country where adequate powers exist to control bank liquidity directly, the principal function of central bank open-market operations should be to influence interest rates, if there is sufficient breadth and regularity of dealings for the impact of the central bank's operations to spread quickly and smoothly throughout the various parts of the market.[3]

Finally, a major obstacle to implementing an appropriate monetary policy (and so an appropriate combination of monetary and budgetary measures) in Australia had been governmental and administrative opposition to flexible interest rates, and this showed signs of passing by 1964. But, on the other hand, it is important that governments should not rely unduly upon monetary measures to prevent excess demand—as they are sometimes inclined to do, especially just before elections—rather than taking budgetary measures, which may be politically more difficult.

It may well be true, nevertheless, that the importance of balance of payments fluctuations in Australia will still present the central bank and the government with more serious problems than those facing, say, the authorities in Britain and the United States. But the extent to which

[3] The ways in which the broader bond market facilitates central bank influence on the economy is admirably described in P. J. Rose, *Australian Securities Markets* (Melbourne, 1969), pp. 3-5.

balance of payments difficulties have overshadowed British policy since World War II, and the attention that even the American authorities have had to give to the balance of payments in recent years in determining their monetary and budgetary policies, makes even this contention less certain than it would have been in earlier decades.

Within the field of monetary policy, up to about 1960 a disproportionate weight was placed upon the quantitative control of bank credit, by comparison with variations in officially controlled interest rates and open market operations (the two other main groups of monetary measures). This is especially strange in view of the difficulties constantly experienced in using direct controls over bank liquidity to secure a speedy reduction in bank lending in Australia, through Statutory Reserve Deposits (or Special Accounts, as they were called up to 1960). The authorities thus almost invariably (until 1964) leaned heavily on the weakest reed among the monetary measures available to them; and by doing so they did not give monetary measures a fair trial. It would thus not be true to say that monetary measures had been tried in Australia and found wanting. It would be more correct to say that at least until 1963–4 they had not really been tried, except in a very limited form, or else too late in each phase of the cycle, when they had proved only too effective—in intensifying cyclical instability.

Variations of interest rates and open-market operations have at any time the advantage that some part of their effect on the liquidity of the public is immediate; whereas quantitative controls over bank credit affect the public only with a considerable lag, when overdrafts available to the public are eventually reduced, and when their unused overdrafts have been utilized as fully as the banks' customers wish.

It has often been said that open-market operations in Australia are difficult because of the narrowness of the bond market. But this is not an obstacle to their use if the aim is to affect the liquidity of the public through changes in asset prices. It is, of course, a drawback if the aim is to affect considerably the liquidity, and so the lending, of the banks through changes in their cash reserves, and so their L.G.S. ratio. But in Australia this effect is usually most readily achieved mainly by the use of S.R.D.s (as we have seen). It is true that the growth of the bond market in recent years has now made it more feasible to make greater use of open-market operations for the purpose of affecting bank liquidity also; and they may well be required for this purpose too, despite the extensive powers that are wielded (at least in theory) by the central bank to control bank liquidity directly. For in practice there may be political or other limitations on the willingness or ability of the central bank to raise S.R.D.s to the requisite level to secure the desired effect on bank lending by this means alone. Moreover, the central bank may sometimes doubt whether the agreed L.G.S. minimum will be adhered to if too great a pressure is placed on bank liquidity by quantitative controls. In any event, if open-market operations are feasible, their immediate impact on the liquidity of the public as well as the banks (in contrast to the delay in the effect on the public of any reduction in bank lending that results from a call to S.R.D.s) constitutes an argument for using open-market operations to some extent to obtain a quick effect and so complement the lagged effects that should follow from the use of direct controls over bank liquidity.

The use of quantitative controls as a means of reducing bank liquidity was up to 1960 usually preferred in Australia to open-market sales, as the latter alternative, even if possible at all on an adequate scale, would have involved considerable reductions in bond prices. There is reason to doubt whether direct controls over bank liquidity are always as effective as open-market operations in securing a given reduction in bank lending with a minimal reduction in bond prices. (In any case, this is not necessarily the right objective.) Analysis of this problem with reference to countries where a cash or liquid assets ratio is the governing one are inconclusive on this point; for the relative effects on bond prices of these alternative ways of securing a given reduction in bank lending will vary with circumstances. In Australia (where an L.G.S. ratio is the principal governing ratio) it will, however, generally be true that, since this amounts to a limitation upon the banks' powers to shift out of bonds into advances, direct controls will normally do less to reduce bond prices than would open-market sales resulting in the same effect on bank lending. However, doubts on this point must arise even in Australia in certain circumstances. In the first place, if one or more banks are operating at above the agreed minimum L.G.S. ratio, scope exists for banks to shift out of bonds into advances, and thus indirectly activate idle balances (by selling the bonds to people with idle balances and lending to those more likely to spend). In the second place, so long as the L.G.S. minimum has not the force of law, there is always the possibility that one or more banks might not adhere to it, or that it might borrow from the central bank on a scale that would enable it to maintain its L.G.S. assets despite the shift in its asset holdings from bonds into advances. In either of these circumstances there may be doubts about which of the two alternatives would have the smaller effect on bond sales (and so on bond prices).

In any case, the policy that has the least effect on bond sales (and therefore, generally, on bond prices) is often not the preferable one. It is then even more likely to be true that the quantitative control of bank lending may be inferior to the use of open-market operations for the same general purpose. In any event, there is reason to believe that a central bank is more likely to obtain the best results—the closest approach to the securing of its various objectives—if it has several policy weapons with which to operate, and if it uses them in various combinations to secure whatever ends it has in mind at any particular time.[4]

The future of S.R.D.s

By the second half of the 1960s the ratio of Statutory Reserve Deposits to bank deposits had been reduced to well below any previous level. This was partly the result of normal releases, but partly also of releases from S.R.D.s in connection with the setting up and the expansion of the Term Loan Fund and the establishment in December 1965 of the Farm Development Loan Fund. The very low level to which S.R.D.s had been reduced naturally raises the issue of how far they would be available for release in future if it were thought necessary to increase bank liquidity.

It would, of course, always be possible to increase bank liquidity in other ways—by running government deficits, by open-market purchases, by loans to the banks on acceptable terms and, indeed, if necessary, by

[4] Cf. A. D. Bain, 'Monetary Control through Open-Market Operations and Reserve Requirement Variations', *Economic Journal*, March 1964.

merely creating more bankers' deposits with the Reserve Bank by a stroke of the pen. But all these courses of action might face real or imagined difficulties when the time came to operate them. Moreover, even short of the point at which their Statutory Reserve Deposits fell to zero, banks might begin to react to the prospect of their disappearance by restraining the growth of their lending, or in other ways that might not be in accord with the needs of the economy at the time. Particularly if different banks reacted in different ways to the possibility of the disappearance of their S.R.D.s this might present certain problems for monetary control. At the very least, one might say that the reduction in S.R.D.s to unprecedentedly low ratios probably strengthens the case for developing and using other weapons of central banking—at least for purposes of expansion.

Operations in the money market as a weapon of central banking

There has since 1959 been an officially backed short-term money market in Australia. The approved (or 'authorized') dealers accept deposits from the public including the banks, and until early 1965 were permitted to hold only a portfolio of short-term government securities (Treasury notes and short-term bonds up to three years from maturity). They were given permission early in 1965 to hold also commercial bills accepted by banks. They have a line of credit available to each of them from the central bank, which was until 1964 limited to a fixed figure which had gradually been increased. In 1964 this limit was removed, but the line of credit available to each dealer was still limited by reference to its capital resources. In 1969 the dealers were granted permission to hold small amounts of a number of other assets (and no longer only commercial bills), and to deal in (that is, to buy and sell) much larger amounts of various assets, including long-term government bonds.

The growth of an officially backed money market was expected to reduce the importance of unofficial dealings of a similar nature, especially in the inter-company loan market and unofficial buy-back operations in government bonds (which are in effect a deposit of cash with a dealer in return for a bond which the dealer promises to buy back at a higher figure at some later date). The more attractive terms for fixed-term deposits that banks were permitted to offer in 1964 and subsequent years were intended also to reduce the relative importance of unofficial money-market dealings. So far as this occurred, it was likely to facilitate central banking, as it reduced the relative importance of those flows of short-term lending over which the Reserve Bank had no direct influence, and about which it probably had inadequate information.[5] Some transfers of funds to the official market probably resulted, but the growth of the official market seems also to have helped to foster habits and contacts that promoted the use of the unofficial outlets for short-term funds.

The regular dealings in short-term bonds by a group of money-market dealers seem to have facilitated open-market operations in early 1964, in the sense that a change of policy by the Reserve Bank towards greater readiness to sell bonds and greater reluctance to buy them was followed by a general rise in the yields of short-term bonds. More irregular falls in the prices of particular issues would probably have occurred in the

[5] It should be borne in mind, however, that it is unforeseen changes in the flow of non-bank credit, rather than its relative importance as such, that is likely to present problems for a central bank.

absence of the body of specialist dealers in these issues. Even where the aim of open-market operations is to affect interest rates, therefore, a relatively broad and active market is an advantage in that the adjustment of bond prices to a new policy is then more likely to be orderly and smooth over the range of interest rates. Similarly, in 1969–70 the increases in short-term bond rates resulting from Reserve Bank policy spread quickly and smoothly to the longer-term maturities, apparently partly as a result of the fact that the dealers were now operating a regular market in longer-term as well as short-term bonds.

If the Reserve Bank is able and willing to affect interest rates in the official short-term money market, by changes in the terms on which it makes cash available to the dealers, whether by loans to them or by purchasing securities they wish to sell, it may reasonably hope to influence the flow (and the cost) of short-term funds to the private sector of the economy. Changes in the official short-term money-market's rates are likely to have some influence on the level of short-term rates in the private capital market. When the rates offered by finance companies and others for notes and short-term debentures are tending to rise, a corresponding upward movement of rates in the official money market and in banks' fixed-interest-bearing deposit rates, and those on Treasury Notes, should reduce the likelihood of idle balances being lent to the private sector. Such a policy should thus dampen down the activation of idle balances, which often acts as a stimulus to a higher level of demand in times of full employment.

Fees on unused overdrafts

Early in 1966 fees (at fairly low rates) were introduced on the unused part of the overdraft limits granted by banks to certain types of borrowers. It seems that this had the effect of causing some of these borrowers to negotiate some reduction in their overdraft limits. One implication of this for central banking might be that there would thus be rather less scope than in earlier booms for borrowers to finance a high level of spending by making fuller use of their overdraft limits, though the fees would probably have to be at a higher rate and have a wider coverage to have any important effect in this direction.[6]

But, on the other hand, if a firm is being charged for having an unused overdraft—especially if the fee is considerable—there is obviously rather more inducement for it to make fuller use of its overdraft limits than there would be if the unused part of the limits was not costing anything. In other words, given the rate charged on overdrafts (that is, the charge for making use of one's overdraft limits), the existence of fees on unused overdrafts would tend to induce borrowers to make fuller use of them, and to that extent might weaken central bank control of borrowing from banks in some future boom. This effect could, however, be offset by raising the rates charged on overdrafts to a higher level than would otherwise have been thought necessary.

But the main aim of permitting the introduction of the fees was apparently to reduce the extent to which firms borrowed on the inter-company loan market using their unused overdrafts as security. The introduction of the fees probably had some effect in this direction so far as concerns small firms or those with relatively low credit-standing, but not upon borrowing by major firms.[7] The existence of the fees might, however, reduce

[6] The case for a commitment fee on unused overdrafts is discussed in an article by Professor H. W. Arndt, 'Overdrafts and Monetary Policy', *Quarterly Review,* Banca Nazionale del Lavoro, Rome, September 1964.

[7] I am indebted for this point to Dr P. J. Rose.

the likelihood of smaller firms being able to expand their borrowing in the inter-company loan market in some future boom, and so limit the extent to which an expansion of this form of non-bank credit might hamper central bank control in such a period.

Direct compared with indirect control over non-bank financial intermediaries

All borrowing and lending in the economy is affected, to a greater or smaller degree, by any successful measures of monetary (or budgetary) policy. The glib assertion is often heard that non-bank financial institutions, especially finance companies, are not controlled by the central bank and that they should therefore be 'controlled'— explicitly or by implication, directly. But this sort of bald assertion is merely a misleading substitute for reasoned discussion of a very complex issue.

In the first place, the part played by the expansion of non-bank credit, especially that provided through finance companies, in recent booms in Australia has often been exaggerated. In the second place, it is not the considerable extent of non-bank credit that limits central bank action; indeed, as some writers have pointed out, in itself a high 'velocity of circulation', a high ratio of non-bank to bank credit, ought to increase the central bank's powers of control over spending, since it means that each unit of the money supply (which the central bank is supposed to be able to control) supports a large superstructure of non-bank credit. What in fact may limit the central bank's powers to curb spending is the expansion of non-bank (relative to bank) credit at a rate it is unable to foresee, or on a scale that may be in part a consequence of its own measures of control over the banking system. Up to a point the central bank should be able to foresee the growth of the importance of non-bank credit in a boom. But it can certainly not foresee the precise forms that growth is most likely to take, and the attempt to control directly particular forms of non-bank credit will tend to stimulate the search for those forms of lending not subject to direct control.

It may nevertheless be conceded that if some forms of direct control over the most important financial intermediaries prove to be possible, their use may well facilitate policy to some extent and should probably do no great harm. But the authorities might then fail to make proper use of the more politically unpopular measures of tighter budgets and higher interest rates, in the hope that they could secure the desired effect on demand by exercising direct controls over those financial intermediaries they could control directly. A further disadvantage would be that the inevitable attempts to avoid the effects of the controls would foster the search for new (and generally less efficient) forms of borrowing and lending not subject to direct control.

The most effective controls would presumably be over the cash or L.G.S. ratios of the intermediaries in question. Powers might reasonably be taken to impose minimum cash ratios on any firm accepting short-term deposits of the same maturities as banks, even if only in order to safeguard the depositors, and to avoid apparent inequity towards banks. But it would be hard to foresee what effect on the lending of non-bank intermediaries would result from a given change in the required ratio; for such intermediaries vary greatly in the ratios they aim at (if, indeed, they have any clear idea of a 'target' ratio). The problem of controlling such a wide and varied range of institutions would thus be appreciably more complex than the similar problem of influencing the policies of Australian banks by ratio control.

In view of all the difficulties, if the aim is to control

consumer borrowing, something like the British control over the terms of hire-purchase contracts (minimum cash deposits and maximum periods of repayment) might be applied. But if the statutory powers were taken (or agreement reached among the states and with the Commonwealth) to enforce such a control in Australia, and if it were then used, it should always be applied in combination with variations in sales-tax on consumer durables—to achieve a comparable effect on sales made for cash—and always in combination with the more general (if more slowly acting) monetary and budgetary measures. For in the countries that have applied controls over the terms of hire-purchase contracts, these seem to have had a large and temporary impact on spending (while the higher deposit is being saved up), and might therefore be thought a useful complement to more general budgetary and monetary measures, which normally operate with a longer lag. It should, however, be borne in mind that the United States authorities found the direct control of consumer credit so hard to operate successfully that they have not used it since the early 1950s, and that its use in Britain has not been an unqualified success and has often stimulated the use of other substitutes for hire-purchase credit, such as rental agreements.

Moreover, those types of financial intermediaries that showed the most rapid growth in the recent past (and which are therefore most likely to be the ones that the authorities would seek to control) may well not do so again. Part of the rise of hire-purchase finance in the booms of the 1950s and the first half of the 1960s was presumably due to once-for-all secular elements, arising from the widespread acceptance of hire-purchase borrowing as socially permissible, and from the acceptance of claims on these companies as being 'liquid':

that is, as fairly close substitutes for claims on banks. (On the other hand, company losses and insolvencies in 1961 and 1962 may well have caused some once-for-all revision of this attitude.) This being so, any detailed controls that might be imposed over one group of institutions (such as finance companies) would serve partly to stimulate the growth of new institutions and new forms of lending, especially those that would in any event be making the running in the next boom. This does not mean that it would serve no useful purpose to try to control certain types of financial intermediaries, but merely that the effectiveness of such controls would be less than expected and constantly in process of being reduced. (The situation would continually 'slip from under the grip of the authorities', as the Radcliffe Report put it.)

Again, part of the trouble in Australia in 1955 and 1960 resulted from the stimulus given to the growth of non-bank intermediaries by the failure of the authorities to raise bank and bond interest rates soon enough and far enough to keep pace with the rising demand for funds; whereas sharper increases would have served to reduce the flow of funds for financing private expenditure. If one could assume these mistakes would not be made yet again, the dimension of the problem would in future be much less, even if not entirely insignificant.

Direct- versus indirect-tax variations[8]

There are clearly administrative difficulties in the way of frequent variations in direct-tax rates during the course of a financial year—despite the flexibility demonstrated in Australia in 1962. There is also some evidence

[8] See J. W. Nevile, *Fiscal Policy in Australia* (Melbourne, 1970), p. 106. Parts of the first paragraph of this section owe much to Nevile; the second paragraph is mildly critical of some of his conclusions on this matter.

that variations in receipts from indirect taxes have proved to be a more powerful tool in Australia. It may also be argued that, if people regard changes in income-tax rates as temporary, they are less likely to adjust their expenditure fully when their disposable incomes fall.[9] For example, they will draw upon their savings to a considerable extent to avoid reducing their expenditure fully in proportion to what they expect to be a temporary reduction in their disposable incomes. On the other hand, if there is a rise in the sales-tax payable on cars, for example, and if the expectation is that this is likely to be temporary, people will usually increase the proportion of their disposable income that they choose to save—pending the reduction in the sales-tax, when they expect to be able to acquire the car at a lower price. Small and frequent changes in indirect-tax rates (*once they are actually made*) are especially likely to lead to these desirable stabilizing effects on expenditure; whereas the effects of small and frequent changes in income-tax rates upon spending are especially likely to be offset by compensating changes in people's savings. But against this one must set the generally undesirable effects that result from the *expectation* that indirect-tax rates may be changed; for this often leads to greatly increased purchases of the relevant items at a time when activity is already high, and to an abrupt curtailment of purchases when the tax rates have been increased. This may occur even if the rates are not increased, once people become convinced that increases are not likely to occur, or when they have already brought forward as much of their purchases of these consumer durables as

[9] The Australian practice during the 1960s of varying income-tax rates by a flat-rate surcharge or rebate, apparently intended to emphasize the temporary nature of the changes, might therefore be held likely to minimize the stabilizing effect on demand of given changes in income-tax rates.

can readily be varied in their timing. Perhaps something can be done to avoid these undesirable effects by making any changes in tax rates relatively small and frequent, not normally at the time of the annual budget, and by varying them before the public comes to expect such changes.

But the frequent variation of sales-taxes on durables on occasions apart from the annual budget (as suggested by Nevile) would not necessarily reduce the likelihood of undesirable fluctuations in the demand for these products; for it might merely mean that speculation on the possibility of changes in the rates would become more frequent. It is true that the smaller they expected such changes to be, and the more varied were people's expectations about the precise timing of such changes, the less would such difficulties be. But it would be hard to convince people that any changes in rates of sales-tax would be small; and if the changes in rates were in fact small, it would be difficult to secure the desired effect on total demand. One may also reasonably be sceptical about the likelihood that governments would generally vary the rates in the appropriate direction *before* the public became convinced that such changes were likely to occur.

Furthermore, even if variations in rates of sales-tax did generally affect the demand for retail sales of finished products in the desired direction, this would not necessarily stabilize the demand for their *output*. For the frequent variations of the relevant tax rates might well lead to very sharp fluctuations in the stocks of these items held by retailers and wholesalers. On balance, therefore, whatever the effects on consumption, the effect on the level of activity would not necessarily be stabilizing. One ought also to take some account of the unsettling and costly effects upon retailers and wholesalers that would result from frequent changes in these tax rates.[10]

For these reasons the present writer would not favour placing greater reliance upon variations in sales-tax on major consumer-durable items as a means of reducing fluctuations in the level of activity. For the purpose of reducing fluctuations in the level of demand it seems more appropriate to use changes in indirect taxes on items of expenditure that cannot readily be postponed or speeded up, and—so far as is administratively feasible—upon varying direct tax rates. If there were an indirect tax levied at a fairly low rate on a very wide range of transactions (such as a tax on value added) this could usefully be varied in such a way as to offset fluctuations in demand. Moreover, variations in such a tax would not have the distorting effect on the pattern of consumption that results from the heavy concentration of tax changes on a few major items. For this emphasis on a few indirect taxes is undesirable in itself, as it leaves consumers with less freedom to choose where they will make the economies in their expenditure than if the tax increases were more broadly based; and the concentration of tax changes upon items of durable consumption that can readily be postponed is especially undesirable, because of the fluctuations in demand that result from the expectations of such changes.

Seasonal fluctuations in liquidity

There are considerable fluctuations from month to month in the liquidity of the public (and the banking system) in Australia as a result of the fluctuations in receipts from particular taxes. (The seasonal fluctuation in export receipts resulting from the dependence upon

[10] I am indebted to Professor R. F. Henderson for discussions on which this paragraph is based.

rural products, which used to be of considerable importance, has dwindled to the point where it is no longer a considerable problem—largely owing to the remarkable rise in the relative importance of minerals and manufactures in total exports.)

The method of collection of company taxes concentrates such payments heavily into the latter part of the financial year, and payments of personal income tax by the self-employed are also mainly in the second half of the financial year, so that the later months tend to be ones of tight liquidity. On the other hand, the concentration of tax refunds (to those whose pay-as-you-earn deductions during the course of the year exceed their tax liabilities as subsequently assessed in the light of their tax returns) into the first half of the financial year brings about a seasonal ease in the capital market during the first half of the financial year (from about August onwards). Such seasonal elements in tax collections are not, of course, peculiar to Australia; but it does seem that the seasonal fluctuations are especially marked, mainly as a result of the relative emphasis and timing and method of collection of certain taxes in Australia.[11]

But the problem of dealing with such seasonal fluctuations seems also to be greater in Australia than in Britain or the United States (at least), by reason of the absence of adequately offsetting seasonal fluctuations in purchases by the public of short-term government securities. One object of introducing Seasonal Treasury Notes in the later 1950s and then Treasury Notes in the 1960s (the government obligations corresponding to

---

[11] This topic is discussed, and a quantitative assessment of it is given, in the *Australian Economic Review*, no. 1, 1970, pp. 4-5. Revisions to the method of company tax payments during 1974/5 seem likely to have greatly reduced this problem.

Treasury bills in other countries) was mainly to absorb this seasonal excess of liquidity. The fact that they have not by any means completely fulfilled this function may be explained by a number of factors.

In the first place, the habit of purchasing and then selling such securities, in accordance with seasonal fluctuations in liquidity, would take time to establish even if the returns on the securities were always attractive; but—more important—the rate of return available on Treasury Notes was throughout much of the 1960s insufficiently attractive to compete with returns available elsewhere (in the inter-company loan market, for instance), and there was a notable absence of willingness to vary the rate in order to maintain its competitiveness. Moreover, there are no securities (like tax reserve certificates in Britain) specially designed for companies to purchase against future tax liabilities.

Whatever the reasons for the seasonal fluctuation in liquidity, it seems to have operated in a manner that often inhibited the appropriate use of monetary policy. For in the months of the year when liquidity was high very substantial sales of government securities would normally have been necessary if a tight monetary policy was to be imposed, and the Reserve Bank might often not possess a portfolio of assets attractive to prospective buyers—at least at the interest rates at which the authorities were willing to see them offered. On the other hand, in the later months of the financial year, existing seasonal stringencies made it easy to enforce a tight money policy, merely by refraining from giving the normally forthcoming seasonal relief by Reserve Bank purchases of bonds. It is no accident that two very clear occasions of the most forthright use of open-market operations in an anti-inflationary direction occurred during the second half of the years 1963/4 and 1969/70.

One may surmise that a greater readiness to allow rates of interest on the relevant government securities to vary in ways that would keep them competitive with the market rates would enable the authorities to offset by their operations a larger part of these seasonal fluctuations; and the introduction of securities providing special incentives for companies with seasonally flush liquidity to purchase them might be a useful way of reducing these fluctuations. But reforms of the tax system that would reduce the seasonal element would be a more satisfactory solution.

At the same time, one might expect that purely seasonal fluctuations in the liquidity of the public should not in themselves have effects on the expenditure of the public; for provided that the seasonal pattern is fairly regular, one might expect this factor to be allowed for in people's expenditure plans (and, indeed, it certainly is allowed for in many cases). The basic difficulty may well be that the precise nature of the seasonal pattern is by no means regular enough to give rise to this sort of natural adjustment. For fluctuations in the relative importance of different types of tax receipts may cause the element of seasonality to vary from year to year; and the remarkable changes in the structure of the Australian economy—or at least in its exports—over the course of the 1960s, and perhaps the effects of drought in some years, may well have made seasonal fluctuations in liquidity harder to predict with accuracy. The difficulty of estimating how much of a given fluctuation is in fact due to purely seasonal factors must make it hard for the Reserve Bank to estimate what seasonal relief it ought to give, and how far it should operate in the reverse direction when liqudity is flush.

In short, if monetary policy is to be available as a weapon of policy that can operate in either direction at any time in the financial year it may well be of importance to find ways of minimizing these difficulties arising out of seasonal fluctuations in liquidity.

Lags

Certain more or less inevitable lags are to be expected before measures of budgetary and monetary policy have their full impact upon spending. There is, first, the period that must elapse before the authorities have adequate data to assess the state of the economy at any given time and to make the best estimate they can of future prospects. This lag can be reduced somewhat by investing in the improvement of the country's statistics, and in collecting, processing and analysing information about businessmen's intentions (even if only by obtaining answers to such simple questions as whether their orders or plans have gone up or down, or remained much the same since the previous survey).

The second lag is the delay between the time when the best estimate has been made of the state of the economy and the time when policy-makers muster resolution to take steps to stimulate or check demand. It should be possible to reduce this lag considerably; and it was this lag that was responsible for most of the errors of macro-economic policy in Australia in 1960-3 (and, indeed, in the two earlier booms). The events of 1963-70 gave some grounds to hope that the delays in implementing appropriate measures of monetary policy that had characterized earlier periods might henceforth be avoided. But the appropriate timing of budgetary measures might well necessitate further progress towards increasing their flexibility.

The two lags so far considered may be termed 'inside' lags. The other—or 'outside'—lag is the period that must elapse between the taking of appropriate policy measures and the date at which they affect spending. This lag will consist of a complex of different lags; for any given measure will have some immediate impact and some long-delayed effects. But the typical (or 'weighted average') effect of a given measure will obviously vary greatly from time to time and from country to country. It may prove to be greatest for monetary measures—as compared with budgetary ones. But we know virtually nothing about the typical lag in Australia for various measures; and it must inevitably be hard to assess such typical lags. Yet it is important to try to do this; if, for example, the typical lag for a certain measure turned out to be as long as half a normal trade cycle, one would actually have to apply expansionary policies at the top of a boom and anti-inflationary policies during a recession—which would scarcely be likely to prove politically feasible.

There is, however, no reason to believe that the typical lag in Australia is as inconveniently long as this. Any monetary measures will have some immediate effect in curbing a boom, though some of their effects may well be delayed a year or more. But this means that they must be taken early in the upswing, and that once the downswing has clearly started (as by mid-1961) they should be swiftly reversed, and expansionary budgetary measures (if these are expected to act more quickly) be introduced to offset the lagged after-effects of the previous anti-inflationary monetary (and budgetary) measures. If the policy lags described earlier can be avoided or reduced, the lag before measures have their effect on spending is not likely to be so long as to cause recessions even as great as that of 1961–2, nor booms as great as that of 1960. Some divergences from full employment (in both directions) would still occur, but they might then vary merely from, say, approximately the state of affairs prevailing from 1957–9 (on the one hand) to that of 1964–6 (on the other).

Capital inflow and monetary control

The then deputy governor of the Reserve Bank pointed in 1965 to the problems that may arise for monetary policy in Australia as a result of borrowing overseas by Australian firms in periods of tight credit, such as that of late 1960.[12] So far as firms prove able to undertake extra overseas borrowing—especially through parent companies in overseas countries—in order to offset the effects upon them of a tightening of bank credit within Australia, this will reduce the downward effect on demand within Australia resulting from the curtailment of lending by Australian banks.

But this argument assumes that the overriding aim of policy in the period in question is to reduce domestic spending. In retrospect, at least, one may doubt whether this should have been the main aim of policy in Australia in the second half of 1960; whereas there can be no doubt that a principal aim of policy at that time should have been to improve the balance of payments; and to this task the extra overseas borrowing clearly contributed. Indeed, monetary policy is sometimes used intentionally for this purpose. One should not, therefore, consider this access to overseas capital as a limitation upon central banking policy except in a period when the balance of payments was already strong, *and* when a state of excess demand prevailed internally. On the other hand, in periods of balance of payments difficulty, especially if this was making the policy-makers hesitant about taking internal measures to stimulate domestic

[12] J. G. Phillips, *Recent Developments in Monetary Policy in Australia,* E. S. and A. Bank Research Lecture, 1964 (Brisbane, 1965), p. 24.

spending, the ready availability of overseas capital would be an unmixed blessing from the viewpoint of both internal and external balance.

Measures to affect relative costs

Even if an appropriate combination of budgetary and monetary measures to attain a given level of total spending should not prove too difficult to achieve in future, there remains the task of reconciling this level of demand with the relative price level that will secure external as well as internal balance.

Whatever the defects of import controls, they did at least constitute an additional weapon that could be employed to facilitate the solution of this dual problem. Their passing in 1960 cannot, however, be regretted by policy-makers, importers or consumers (or by most other observers of the economic scene). In any case their continued absence from the armoury must be assumed to be likely for the foreseeable future, partly on practical grounds and partly because Australia's international commitments make it doubtful whether they could be restored in anything short of a major crisis. (They could, in any event, do nothing to eliminate a balance of payments surplus—unless, of course, they had previously been imposed, so that they could then be removed.)

This means that other weapons affecting the relative price level here and abroad will have to be used if the monetary and budgetary weapons do not succeed in achieving a level of demand that secures both internal and external balance.

It is possible that variations in the mix of monetary and budgetary measures could be used, to a limited extent, for maintaining simultaneous internal and external balance. For example, if in a period of excess demand there was a choice between a package of monetary measures on the one hand, and one of budgetary measures on the other, each of which was expected to have about the same effect in restraining demand, the choice might reasonably fall on the monetary measures if there was at the same time an external deficit; for the higher interest rates would tend to increase capital inflow, whereas a tighter budget would normally reduce interest rates (and so tend to reduce capital inflow). But if the initial state of excess demand was accompanied by an external surplus, the case for using budgetary measures, rather than monetary ones, to restrain demand would be stronger.

Indeed, it has been argued that monetary measures should be directed mainly at maintaining external balance so long as exchange rates are fixed and if international capital flows are very responsive to interest-rate dfiferentials; whilst budgetary measures should be directed towards maintaining internal balance. This might, however, mean that in periods of less than full employment and external deficit interest rates would actually have to be raised—the unhelpful effect of this action upon domestic demand having to be offset by making the budget even more expansionary than would otherwise have been necessary. But one may doubt whether in practice budgetary measures could generally be made flexible enough to carry all the weight of maintaining internal balance in the face of monetary measures pulling at times in the opposite direction.

In fact, the scope for varying the mix of budgetary and monetary measures to achieve both internal and external balance (without the use of the exchange rate or some comparable measure) is likely in practice to be severely limited. For one thing, the favourable effect of higher interest rates upon capital inflow is likely to be mainly temporary and once-for-all, while the net inflow is being adjusted to the new level of interest rates (whereas measures to improve the balance of payments by curtailing domestic demand or by the use of the exchange rate will have much more lasting effects). Moreover, the level of interest rates that has to be established if external and internal balance are to be achieved at a fixed exchange rate may conflict with that which is considered desirable from certain other viewpoints, such as the domestic distribution of income or the allocation of resources. Or the greater dependence on capital inflow resulting from higher interest rates may itself be considered undesirable. Once one takes into account additional policy objectives such as these a further policy instrument is therefore required—preferably the exchange rate—even if variations in the mix of monetary and budgetary measures can be used to some extent to achieve simultaneous internal and external balance. It seems unlikely, therefore, that a high degree of success in achieving macro-economic objectives can generally be expected—especially if other aims of economic policy have also to be considered—without a readiness to make appropriate use of the exchange rate.

Rules of thumb versus 'fine-tuning' or 'zig-zagging'

If there are considerable delays before a government intervenes to affect the level of demand in the desired direction or before policy measures have their main effect, there is clearly a risk that the measures adopted may make things worse rather than better. The anti-inflationary measures taken in Australia in 1951, 1956 and 1960 were all good examples of measures that were probably so timed that their main effect was in the direction of worsening the subsequent lapse from full employment.

The frequent failures of governments to act at the right time has led an eminent American economist, Milton Friedman, to advocate that they should refrain from frequent small adjustments of policy ('fine-tuning' or 'zig-zagging') and should aim instead at bringing about a steady growth of the money supply and of government spending and tax receipts (so far as possible). His argument is that the results of applying such a rule of thumb would be preferable to those achieved in many countries in the past by policy variations that were intended to be stabilizing. He suggests that governments should aim at bringing about an annual rate of growth of the money supply related to the trend rate of growth in the real capacity of the economy (perhaps about 5½ per cent per annum for Australia) plus an allowance for the rate of inflation that the country considers tolerable (which might be 2½ to 3 per cent per annum for Australia).

In the United States (which Friedman has chiefly in mind) an additional lag before appropriate measures can be taken is liable to occur as a result of the need for the Administration—once it is itself convinced of the need for action—to convince Congress that changes in tax rates or in government expenditure are desirable. In Australia this particular problem is not present: as soon as the government is convinced of the need for action it can usually take it without further delay. So far as the case for refraining from 'fine-tuning' in the United States rests on these special difficulties, the case is therefore a weaker one in Australia.

In any event, even the adoption of rules of thumb for monetary policy involves the use of discretion in one form or another. A decision has to be taken about the exact definition of the money supply that is to be used. (Should it include interest-bearing deposits with trading banks, and savings bank accounts, as well as current accounts and currency?) It would also be necessary to decide what is the appropriate rate of growth in the money supply, and under what conditions this rate should be revised. Moreover, some departures from a rigidly fixed rate of growth would on occasions be desirable, and perhaps more defensible in Australia than in the United States; for, in particular, in Australia the capacity of the economy may be sharply reduced by drought in certain years, and this may make it defensible in such periods to allow a slower rise in the money supply than in average years. Furthermore, the influence of the balance of payments on the money supply is much larger in Australia than in the United States: so that even if monetary and budgetary policies are such as to permit excess demand, the rate of increase in the money supply may still be fairly steady; for at overfull employment imports are likely to rise sharply, and the resulting balance of payments deficit will reduce the growth of the money supply.

The most useful lesson to be learned from the Friedman approach is probably that policy-makers should have in the back of their minds a 'target' rate of growth of the money supply, from which the actual rate of increase should not be allowed to depart very much unless there were very convincing reasons for the departure. They would then be much less likely to permit dangerously high rates of increase in the money supply, such as have often occurred in times of boom, when a central bank was supporting the bond market with one hand while it was squeezing bank lending with the other. Similarly, in recessions, if a reasonably steady growth in the money supply can be achieved, the recession is not likely to become very deep.

As a matter of fact, during most of the latter part of

the 1960s the annual rates of increase in the money supply in Australia were kept within a reasonably small margin of the trend rate of increase of about 8½ per cent per annum, with the velocity of circulation rising in periods of high activity, so that the growth of the money supply was sufficient to support a more rapidly rising level of activity in such periods. One should not conclude from this that the shadow of Milton Friedman was necessarily lurking somewhere in the Reserve Bank, but merely that some of the more extreme errors of policy that Friedman (and others) have reasonably critized in the United States and Britain during the same period were avoided in Australia during most of the 1960s (though not, as we have seen, in a number of earlier periods).

But it seems unnecessary and undesirable to go further than keeping a watch on the annual rates of increase in the money supply, and to adopt the Friedman prescription of aiming at a strictly controlled annual rate of growth. To abandon all reasonable discretion in such policy matters would be to jettison the baby with the bath-water. Friedman has a reasoned—though probably excessive—scepticism about the ability of policy-makers to vary their budgetary and monetary measures at the appropriate time; and it has to be admitted that Australians might reasonably have shared that scepticism on the basis of many of the policy decisions made in the 1950s and the early part of the 1960s. But the performance of the policy-makers between 1963 and 1970 was such as to justify a certain degree of confidence in their judgment and in their ability to affect demand in the right way at about the right time (even when all due allowance has been made for the favourable external circumstances prevailing during the period).

It is, however, of interest to observe that the one occasion in the later years of the 1960s when their judgment was somewhat at fault was about the year 1966, when for a time the money supply rose a good deal less rapidly than its trend rate of growth, and when the economy lapsed from full employment for a while. At the same time, even if the aim had been to bring about a rather faster rise in the money supply at that time it might have been difficult to achieve it. This exemplifies one of the problems with the Friedman approach: namely that the growth of demand and that of the money supply affect each other, and in varying degrees. For example, in a recession banks may find relatively few borrowers that they regard as creditworthy, and may therefore not raise the level of bank lending (and so the money supply) as fast as the monetary authorities would wish, and as fast as their liquidity position would permit. Many influences other than policy thus affect the rate of growth of *both* the level of demand *and* the supply of money. The use of a simple rule of thumb can therefore be criticized on the grounds that it may be difficult to apply.[13]

Finally, even if the application of rules of thumb did succeed better than fine-tuning in keeping the economy close to full employment, there is still the problem of external balance—which generally bulks larger for Australia than for the United States. Friedman's policy prescriptions would include the adoption of freely fluctuating exchange rates; and if this were done, the problem of external balance would cease to exist. But, in practice,

---

[13] The effects of a given rise in the money supply may differ according to the way in which it occurs (for example, whether it is by way of a budget deficit, or by official bond purchases, or a rise in bank lending, or a balance of payments surplus). But we know too little about any such differences to take much account of this in practice.

even if there is a movement towards rather more ex-
change-rate flexibility than there has been of late (and
this is both likely and probably desirable), it seems certain
to be very much less than Friedman would advocate. It
will therefore still, for the foreseeable future, be necessary
to vary all the instruments of macro-economic
policy—budgetary, monetary and exchange rate—with
judgment and discretion within the feasible limits, in order to attain as close an approximation as possible to internal and external balance.

Conclusion

The experience gained by Australia during the 1950s
and early 1960s in the problems and policies of
achieving and maintaining internal and external balance
provided a sound basis for the generally more successful
policies of the later 1960s. It is true that even the
deficiencies of policy were only relative—relative, that
is, to the exacting aims of policy (by any past standards)
that a modern economy quite rightly sets itself. By comparison with the very high levels of unemployment and
serious balance of payments deficits of the 1930s (and
earlier) the performance during the post-war period was
of course a triumphant success. But by the standards of
the post-war era, the record was a mixed one. From
about 1963–4 onwards, however, it seemed that the
lessons of earlier failures to apply appropriate monetary
measures had been learned. There was rather more
evidence of progress throughout the period towards
making budgetary policy more flexible. But there was no
indication that either the authorities or public opinion
generally were aware of the need to find some appropriate measure directed primarily at influencing the
relationship between domestic and overseas prices to
replace the weapon of import controls, which had been
used for this purpose in the fifties.

II. Lessons from the experience
of 1970 to 1974

The experience of the years 1970–4 bore out many of the lessons that should have been learned from the 1950s and 1960s, especially about the dangers of maintaining inappropriate interest rates and an insufficiently flexible exchange rate. Had the lessons of earlier years been digested and applied during the period Australia need not have experienced as high a rate of inflation as in fact occurred and would probably have been able to enjoy higher and more stable rates of growth and higher living standards.

But the new combination of unemployment with high rates of inflation in the world economy, together with more flexible exchange rates and more mobile international flows of capital in the world generally, made it still more imperative to apply the lessons that earlier experience should have taught policy-makers in Australia, and to apply them in ways that took account of the changing economic environment.

In particular, the events of 1972 and 1974 showed that the rate of inflation could no longer be expected to decline reasonably quickly to tolerable levels as a result of a fairly small rise in unemployment. The combination of high rates of inflation with levels of unemployment far higher than had been experienced before at uncomfortably high rates of inflation meant that it was no longer sufficient merely to vary the general setting of budgetary and monetary measures in the appropriate direction whenever inflation became rapid or unemployment too high. A careful choice had now to be made between the various budgetary and monetary measures in order to ensure that when a stimulus to expansion was required, this was applied in the manner that was least likely to increase cost-push inflation. This meant that there was an especially strong case for reductions in tax rates (especially those affecting the costs of businesses or the take-home pay of wage and salary earners, so far as they were likely to take such rates of tax into account in making their wage demands), rather than for applying the desired stimulus by a higher level of government spending; and, similarly, that when restraint in total demand was needed, the more this was done by reductions in government spending the less would be the need for higher tax rates, and so the less the risk of giving a further stimulus to cost-push inflation.

Superficially one might perhaps think that higher interest rates would tend also to have cost-push effects. But in fact the widespread fallacy to this effect is probably the most serious obstacle to achieving a policy mix that will reduce the rate of inflation at any given level of activity. For holding down interest rates involves having a money supply larger than would otherwise have been necessary; and the larger the money supply (and the lower therefore are nominal interest rates) at any given level of activity, the faster will the price level rise (other things being equal). Nominal interest rates will come down automatically once inflation is checked. But trying to hold interest rates down with a view to stopping inflation is like trying to reduce one's waistline by merely tightening one's belt. Once the waistline has been reduced, and only then, is it safe and sensible for the belt to be tightened.

The political and psychological obstacles to a national interest rate policy seem to be still paralleled in Australia—though not generally now in most other developed countries—by a failure to let the exchange rate adjust in a timely manner, especially in an upward direction. For from the early 1970s onwards exchange rates between major currencies became much more flexible, in contrast to the system that had prevailed since World War II of keeping rates generally fixed but altering them occasionally by large amounts. But from about 1972 the governments of most major countries left the day-to-day movements of their exchange rates to be determined to a much greater extent by market forces (though with varying degrees of official intervention). The resulting system of frequent small adjustments made it in practice much easier for the countries using this system to vary the setting of this major weapon of macro-economic policy than it had been when rates were generally adjusted only rarely. This greater freedom may well have been misused at times; and some would argue that the ease with which currencies could now depreciate in the foreign exchange markets weakened the determination of governments to resist inflation, as they had now become less anxious about its possible adverse balance of payments effects. But the much greater general flexibility of exchange rates meant that there were no longer the severe international currency 'crises' that had occurred so often up to the early 1970s as a result of governments trying to maintain unrealistic exchange rates.

Until September 1974 Australia elected to keep the day-to-day rate for her currency fixed in terms of the U.S. dollar (though this fixed rate was itself changed on several occasions, such as December 1972 and February 1973). This meant that if the daily fluctuations that were occurring in the relative values of major currencies were such that the U.S. dollar was tending to depreciate, the Australian dollar was in fact depreciating to a similar extent—without any decision being taken by the Australian government as to whether this was an appropriate macro-economic measure for Australia. During the first half of 1973, in particular, this brought about an effective depreciation of the Australian dollar (in terms of the average of other currencies) which almost certainly would have been best avoided.

The method adopted by Australia in September 1974 for fixing the exchange rate was to keep it constant in terms of some weighted average (or 'basket') of major currencies (the composition of which was not published), and to quote the resulting rate for the Australian dollar against major currencies each day in the light of this principle. It remained true, therefore, that Australia was retaining a form of fixed exchange rate, and thereby denying herself the fully flexible use of this vital weapon of macro-economic policy, in the sense that major political decisions were still required for any important variation to be made in it. The deficiency of such a system was admirably illustrated by the aftermath of the decision to devalue in September 1974, which was widely criticized—with justice—as being premature and excessive if not totally unnecessary. But under any form of fixed-exchange-rate system a prompt reversal of such an error was politically far more difficult than if a more flexible system of setting it, such as most countries now employ, had been in existence.

It is important that the exchange rate should be variable at least as readily as the setting of monetary and budgetary measures, even if the full available degree of flexibility is not used. This would be facilitated if Australia developed a foreign exchange market in which the rate would vary to a large extent with the state of her international transactions; but, alternatively, an arrangement, which might work as well, or at least be easier to introduce initially, would be for the Reserve Bank to operate in a similar manner to a foreign exchange market, fixing the rate (which could still be in terms of a weighted average of major currencies) from day to day, with the aim of seeing that the country's reserves did not vary outside certain broad limits (which could be varied from time to time by government decision).

It is true that the Labor government proved more flexible than its predecessor in making upward adjustments to the exchange rate, in December 1972 and September 1973. (It also made the one ill-judged adjustment downwards—which had in any case always been the politically easy direction—in September 1974.) But the need to insulate Australia from the rapidly rising rate of world inflation meant that belated upward adjustments such as that of September 1973 were inadequate to deal with the contemporary problem. A country with as open an economy as Australia must be ready to let its exchange rate appreciate at the same rate as inflation occurs in the outside world if it is to insulate itself from world inflation. That alone would not of course be a sufficient prescription for a policy to avoid inflation. For events in Australia may well also be a source of the country's inflation. But it will always be true that outside inflation can never reasonably be blamed for inflation with Australia, for the import of inflation from the rest of the world could always be avoided by a sufficient appreciation. Of course, adjustments of the Australian exchange rate may also be appropriate for other reasons—a sharp change in export prospects or the outlook for capital inflow, for example. But if there is inflation in the rest of the world at a rate in excess of that which would be brought about by economic forces originating within Australia, the correct policy prescription is to revalue upwards by correspondingly more (or to devalue by less) than other considerations would necessitate.

Just as keeping the exchange rate as far in the direction of appreciation (and of avoiding devaluation) as possible will help to restrain the rate of inflation at any given level of activity, in the same way the rate of price increase will be moderated if tariffs can be reduced, or if subsidies can be used instead to assist Australian industries that are deemed to need assistance. But a rational reduction or elimination of tariffs appears to be even more difficult politically than a rational use of the exchange rate and interest rates. This being so, the general reduction in tariffs by 25 per cent in July 1973 (coupled with certain other subsequent tariff reductions) was an especially praiseworthy experiment in using for a macro-economic purpose a revision of tariffs that was probably in any event desirable, even though it may in retrospect have been effected too sharply. It might, indeed, be argued that these tariff reductions were, on allocation of resources grounds, a superior measure to an appreciation; and if one takes this view one would to that extent be able to defend the effective depreciation of the Australian dollar that had occurred (through the rigid tie to the U.S. dollar) during the preceding months, and so helped to make the tariff cuts possible. Unfortunately, a good deal of misguided criticism was subsequently made of these tariff cuts, especially in 1974 when their full effect was felt upon imports and so upon import-competing industries. But criticism would have been much more appropriately directed at the government's failure to maintain an adequate level of total demand in the economy in 1974 and to implement quickly enough adequate schemes to re-train and re-settle employees who had to find alternative employment as a result of the tariff cuts.

The outcries of the highly organized vested interests of the import-competing industries that can point to the creation of 'unemployment' in their industries make it difficult to avoid confusion in the public mind between the loss of jobs in those particular industries and a rise in the general level of unemployment—which ought to be tackled by general macro-economic measures and not by protecting uneconomic industries from imports.

The level of tariffs and subsidies therefore requires to be co-ordinated with budgetary, monetary and exchange rate measures to achieve internal and external balance with a minimum rate of inflation at a given level of activity. But if this is done a closer approximation to these aims should be possible than Australia achieved in 1970–4. Prices and incomes policies may or may not be an appropriate supplement to other macro-economic instruments. But at the very least, a government need not and should not exercise its influence in the direction of making wage-push inflation worse at a time when serious inflation is already in prospect. Yet by its active encouragement of large wage and salary increases in the public sector and its advocacy before the Arbitration Commission of considerable wage increases in 1973 the government certainly made the inflation of 1973–4 worse than it need have been. By the turn of the year 1974–5, however, this lesson appeared to have been learned by at least some senior ministers, who were by then publicly urging wage restraint.

It remains an open question how much can be done to restrain inflation directly by some form of prices and incomes policy. But one can say with confidence that no such policies will work successfully for long if the setting of the other macro-economic instruments is inappropriate: if nominal interest rates are kept so low that real returns to the lender are actually negative; if tax rates are too high; if the exchange rate is such that the currency is allowed to become undervalued; if tariffs are high (and if the superior alternative of subsidies is hardly used at all); and if capital inflow is kept artificially low. Each of the main macro-economic instruments was set incorrectly in these directions for a considerable part of the years 1970–4. Success in the achievement of macro-economic aims in subsequent years will depend largely on whether the lessons that should have been learned from these years about the appropriate mix of policy measures are correctly applied in the future.

Bibliographical Note

Footnotes to the text refer to books and similar sources relating to particular topics raised in the course of this study. Surveys of the economy are available in the regular series of articles in the *Economic Record* from 1956 to 1967, and in the *Australian Economic Review* from 1968 onwards.

The authors and the issues of the *Economic Record* covering the period from 1960 onwards are as follows:

Ian Bowen, August 1960
Kingsley Laffer, December 1960
P. H. Karmel, March 1961
A. R. Hall, September 1961
H. F. Lydall, March 1962
J. O. N. Perkins, September 1962
K. Hancock, March 1963
H. R. Edwards and N. T. Drane, September 1963
E. A. Boehm, March 1964
B. L. Johns, September 1964
R. C. Gates and H. M. Kolsen, March 1965
A. R. Hall, September 1965
G. T. Bills, June 1966
D. S. Ironmonger, June 1967
F. G. Davidson, December 1967

Other surveys of the economy or of matters covered in this study are as follows; the author and the publication, but not the title of the article, are given.

1961   A. D. McKee, *Banker*, January 1961

D. C. Rowan, *Bankers' Magazine*, June and September 1961

R. F. Henderson, *Economic Record*, June and September 1961

G. D. McColl, *Bankers' Magazine*, September 1961

J. D. S. Macleod, *Banker*, November 1961

J. O. N. Perkins, *London and Cambridge Bulletin*, December 1961

1962   J. D. S. Macleod, *Banker*, June 1962

1963   H. W. Arndt, *Banker*, April 1963

R. W. Davis and R. H. Wallace, *Australian Economic Papers*, June 1963

K. Bieda, *Economic Record*, September 1963

J. O. N. Perkins, *Banker*, October 1963

1964   J. D. S. Macleod, *Bankers' Magazine*, June 1964

1965   J. O. N. Perkins, *London and Cambridge Bulletin*, March 1965

A. R. Hall, *Bankers' Magazine*, October 1965

J. O. N. Perkins, *Bankers' Magazine*, October 1965

P. J. Rose, *Bankers' Magazine*, October 1965

D. Cochrane, *Banker*, November 1965

1966   J. O. N. Perkins, *Bankers' Magazine*, December 1966

The following references should also be consulted:

The annual *Reports* of the Reserve Bank of Australia.

The annual White Papers on the Australian Economy.

The regular surveys in bulletins of the various Australian banks.

M. J. Artis and R. H. Wallace, 'Assessing Fiscal Impact', 'A Historical Survey of Australian Fiscal Policy', both in N. Runcie (ed.), *Australian Monetary and Fiscal Policy: selected readings*. London, 1971.

Commonwealth of Australia, *Report of the Committee of Economic Enquiry* (Vernon Report), 2 vols. Canberra, 1965, chapters 2 and 10.

J. E. Isaac, 'Incomes Policy: unnecessary? undesirable? impracticable?', *Australian Economic Review*, 1, 1973.

J. W. Nevile, 'Discretionary Fiscal Policy in Australia, 1955 to 1970', in J. W. Nevile and D. W. Stammer (eds), *Inflation and Unemployment*. Harmondsworth: Pelican, 1972.

J. P. Nieuwenhuysen, 'Wages Policy in Australia: a review of the 1960's', reprinted in J. W. Nevile and D. W. Stammer (eds), *Inflation and Unemployment*.

Organization for Economic Co-operation and Development, *Australia*. Paris, 1972, 1973.

J. G. Phillips, 'Developments in Monetary Theory and Monetary Policy', *R. C. Mills Memorial Lecture*, University of Sydney, 1971. Reprinted in N. Runcie (ed.), *Australian Monetary and Fiscal Policy*.

—— *Recent Developments in Monetary Policy in Australia*, E. S. & A. Bank Research Lecture, 1964. Brisbane, 1965.